MARYLAND
Off the Beaten Path

MARYLAND
Off the Beaten Path

by Judy and Ed Colbert

A Voyager Book

The
Globe
Pequot
Press

Chester, Connecticut

Cover art of skipjack by M. A. Dube
Maps by Ed Colbert
Text art by Carole Drong

Library of Congress Cataloging–in–Publication Data

Colbert, Judy.
    Maryland: off the beaten path/by Judy and Ed Colbert — 1st ed.
        p.   cm.
    "A Voyager Book."
    Includes index.
    ISBN 0–87106–483–9
    1. Maryland—Description and travel—1981—Guide-books.
    I. Title
    F179.3.C65 1990
    917.5204'43—dc20
                                        90–36465
                                         CIP

Manufactured in the United States of America
First Edition/First Printing

Contents

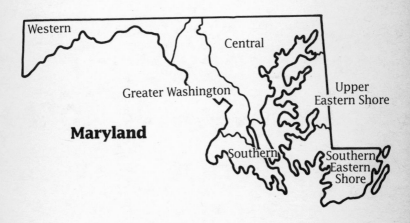

Greetings!

I encourage all Maryland travelers to explore and enjoy <u>Maryland: Off The Beaten Path</u>.

Maryland is one of the most fascinating places in America. It is the ideal place for any vacation. There is something here for everyone: rolling green mountains in Western Maryland, sandy beaches on the Eastern Shore, and many historic sites and special attractions in between. Sports lovers will enjoy a host of activities including boating, fishing, skiing, and whitewater rafting. Fairs and festivals spotlight every town. Whatever your interests, there is plenty to discover in Maryland.

Maryland's beauty takes on a whole new light during each seasonal change -- dogwoods and daffodils in the spring, black-eyed Susans (our state flower) in the summer, and beautiful orange and red foliage in the fall. Scenic routes are well-marked, and many places in Maryland are accessible by public transportation and have provisions for the handicapped.

This guide can lead you on an unforgettable journey. Along the way, you will find many unique perspectives and interesting people. As I travel around the state, I become more and more convinced that the friendliest, most caring people in the world live in Maryland.

Follow <u>Maryland: Off The Beaten Path</u>, and capture a memory to last a lifetime.

William Donald Schaefer
Governor

Mt. Savage Castle

Introduction

Maryland is known by several nicknames, including the Free State, the Old Line State, and America in Miniature; it also is known for its symbols.

If you asked Marylanders why they call it the Free State (road signs say *Keep the Free State Litter Free*), they would probably cite the freedom of worship advocated by the state's founders. Others might point to Maryland's alliance with the northern states during "the war" and its intolerance of slavery. These historical facts are true, but they are not the source of the name. It dates from 1917, when Maryland opposed prohibition on the grounds that it was an issue to be decided by each state.

In 1776, General William Smallwood (1732–92) led the battalion covering the Continental army's retreat at the Battle of Long Island. The Maryland line fought courageously but lost about a third of its men. Because of their stalwart effort, George Washington referred to the Maryland troops as the Old Line.

Maryland is America in Miniature because of its diverse terrain, which stretches from the mountains to the seashore. The mountains are not high compared to the Rockies (Backbone Mountain in Garrett County is the tallest, at 3,360 feet), but they provide fair downhill and excellent cross-country skiing. The seashore is among the finest in the East, including the recently renewed beaches at Ocean City.

Minute quantities of gold have been found along the Potomac, near Great Falls, and in the Piedmont regions of Howard, Montgomery, Frederick, Carroll, Baltimore, and Harford counties. Stop by the Chesapeake and Ohio (C & O) Canal Park and Great Falls Tavern Museum, near the intersection of MacArthur Boulevard and Great Falls Road. Park in the C & O Canal parking area and follow the unmarked trail to the Maryland Gold Mine, which was worked until the 1920s. The shaft and mine area are visible, and a marker tells their story. No one has become rich on Maryland gold, but one can try. For more information about the history of gold finds and prospecting regulations in the state, write to the Maryland Geological Survey, 2300 St. Paul Street, Baltimore 21218.

Not everything in Maryland, however, is miniature. The National Aquarium in Baltimore is one of the world's largest. The collection at the Walters Art Gallery, also in Baltimore, is world renowned.

Maryland has many symbols. Maryland has a state tree (the Wye Oak), a state song ("Maryland, My Maryland" by James Ryder Randall), and a state crustacean (the blue crab). The state bird is the Baltimore oriole, and provisions have been made for its protection. If you can not find orioles in the wild, check Memorial Stadium. In 1988 the Orioles were almost given up for dead, but in 1989 they made a miraculous comeback.

The black-eyed susan is the official flower, and you will see it blooming profusely by the side of the road and in wild-flower beds from late spring through fall.

The state also has an official fossil, the four-ribbed snail, an extinct invertebrate that ranged in size from microscopic to 3 or 4½ inches in diameter. Fossils can be found at the Cliffs of Calvert, in the Choptank, and St. Mary's areas.

Go by the Bay and watch the hunters at work, and frequently you will find Chesapeake Bay retrievers with them, for they are a native-bred amphibious hunter. There was a ban on catching striped bass, or rockfish, during the last four years of the 1980s, but they are back on the list and there is not a sweeter-tasting fish than baked striped bass.

The state sport is jousting, which might invoke images of knights in shining armor; it is the oldest equestrian sport in the world. Like other sports and competitions (such as the rodeo), jousting originated as a test of man's occupational skills. In Maryland, the challenge in jousting is not to toss a man off his horse, but to spear a series of metal rings while riding on a horse. Both men and women compete in this sport. The 80-yard course has three arches from which rings are suspended; in each round, the size of the rings decreases. These are not huge rings to begin with: The largest is 1¾ inches in diameter and the smallest is ¼ inch.

There are numerous jousting tournaments throughout the year. The schedule usually starts in April and continues through to the Maryland State Championship and the

Nationals in October. Events may take place in Hagerstown, Frederick, St. Mary's City, Easton, Denton, Trappe, Port Republic, Lily Pons, Clear Spring, Chestertown, and Havre de Grace. Of course, each tournament has its pageantry and fun, its food and partying. Usually there is an admission charge, which often is used to benefit a charitable organization. Write to the Maryland Jousting Tournament Association, 328 Bush Chapel Road, Aberdeen 21001 for a schedule of events.

Whatever name you know the state by, whatever you want to do here, you will find abundant diversions for the traveler in Maryland. In researching and preparing this book, we avoided the most common attractions and sought the slightly offbeat, the friendly, the tasty, the visually perfect and imperfect, and the most creative sites. We hope you enjoy reading and using our book as much as we enjoyed discovering *Maryland Off the Beaten Path.*

The prices and rates listed in this guidebook were confirmed at press time. We recommend, however, that you call establishments before traveling to obtain current information.

Off the Beaten Path in Western Maryland

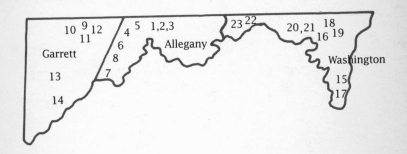

1. Constitution Park
2. Victorian Historic District
3. Allegany Central Railroad
4. Old Depot Center
5. Mt. Savage Castle
6. National Pike Mural
7. Westvaco Paper Company
8. Lonaconing Iron Furnace
9. Casselman Hotel
10. Casselman Bridge
11. Spruce Forest Artisan Village
12. Fuller-Baker Log House
13. Deep Creek Lake
14. Gordon Douglas Boat Company
15. Valley Craft Network
16. Beaver Creek House
    Bed and Breakfast
17. Maple Tree Campground
18. Washington County Museum
    of Fine Art
19. Hagerstown Post Office
    Murals
20. Wilson Village Old General Store
21. Historic Wilson Bridge Picnic Area
22. Park-N-Dine
23. Sideling Hill

Western Maryland

Western Maryland's three counties—Garrett, Allegany, and Washington—are a combination of farmlands, rugged mountains, sedate streams, and white-water rivers. In the eighteenth century, rivers and mountains combined to halt the flow of settlers from the east and from the central part of Pennsylvania. The streams and fertile lands persuaded them to linger. The annual snowfall, subsequent spring melt, and years of forestation deposited an extraordinarily rich soil.

The products of farms and iron furnaces needed to be transported to customers between Wheeling, West Virginia, and the East Coast. So through this territory came the National Pike, which now is Route 40-48. It was the first toll road across the country funded by the federal government. This was long before President Eisenhower dictated there would be a national system of interstate highways. Along the road are many of the original mile markers, white metal (although they look like stone) obelisks that stand about 3 feet high. At LeVale (Allegany) you will find the only remaining tollhouse.

Paralleling the Potomac River to Cumberland was the Chesapeake and Ohio Canal. The canal was George Washington's dream of a water system that would unite the Atlantic with the Ohio River. Traces of the canal, the locks, and the accompanying settlements remain.

Railroads superceded the canal as an efficient means of transportation. Today Interstate 81 and Interstate 70 provide the lifelines connecting this part of the state with the rest of the country. Mountains block vehicles from making a straight westward trip. That is why Interstate 70 heads north at Hancock to meet the Pennsylvania Turnpike, rather than directly west to West Virginia and Ohio.

The geographic features that isolated this part of the state have made it attractive to vacationers; residents from Washington and Baltimore traditionally have come here to escape the summer heat. Washington County is populated by commuters to eastern cities, and its identity with the other western counties has weakened.

Here you will find traces of the Amish and Scottish, of hardy stock, and friendly people. You will note some wealth, both in property and in cultural heritage. As yet, you will not find hundreds of thousands of tourists. You will find hospitality, tranquility, perseverance, a dedication to remember the "old ways," and beautiful mountain scenery.

Allegany County

Outdoor enthusiasts enjoy Allegany County and Cumberland, the county seat. Within the county borders are Rocky Gap State Park, Green Ridge State Forest, and the C & O Canal National Historic Park where people can hunt, boat, fish, camp, and explore history (including historic cemeteries).

Cumberland is considered the mibster capitol of the country. For some reason, the marble players of this town far surpass the players from other towns. A recent world champion was a twelve-year-old from Cumberland. If it has been a while since you played, or if you have never tried, visit **Constitution Park.** In addition to the Little League baseball field, picnic groves, swimming pool, wading pool, playground, railroad caboose, 1937 fire truck, army tank, horseshoe pits, and courts for basketball, tennis, shuffleboard, volleyball, and badminton, there are two game areas with three marble rings each. Games and tournaments are held regularly at the park; six national marble champions have played and practiced here on their way to victory.

Constitution Park is off Williams Street in the southeast area of Cumberland. From Maryland Avenue, turn left on Williams Street to the park entrance. Call (301) 759–6440.

A brochure is available to help you walk through the **Victorian Historic District** of Cumberland, beginning at the western property line of 630 Washington Street and extending east to the east bank of Wills Creek. The brochure highlights the architectural details and historical importance of about three dozen buildings.

The Western Maryland Station Center, which was in service from 1913 until 1976, is now a museum dedicated to the history of railroading in this part of the country. The center houses the Allegany County tourism office, the Allegany Arts

Council, the Allegany Central Railroad, the C & O Canal National Park office, and an Industrial and Transportation Museum and Cultural Center.

Exhibits in the museum highlight the railroad, the National Pike (the first federal toll highway constructed across the country), the C & O Canal (a full-size lock is included in the exhibits), and local industries such as brewing and distilling, iron making, glass making, tire making (Kelly-Springfield), and mining. Mercantile establishments and the local First and Last Chance Saloon are represented as well.

The Allegany Arts Council has twenty-four arts organizations actively involved in choral singing, theater, cinema, photography, crafts, instrumental music, and visual arts. Classes are scheduled regularly and a gallery exhibits works that are for sale. The Canal Visitor's Center has an interpretive display in the station, where photographs, models, and artifacts are exhibited.

The Industrial and Transportation Museum is open Tuesday through Sunday from 11:00 A.M. to 4:00 P.M. The Allegany Arts Council is open Monday through Friday from 9:00 A.M. to 3:00 P.M., and their telephone is (301) 777–9137. The C & O Canal National Park is open on Tuesday from 11:00 A.M. to 4:00 P.M.; Wednesday through Saturday 10:00 A.M. to 5:00 P.M.; and Sunday 1:00 to 4:00 P.M. The Allegany County tourism office is open Monday through Friday from 8:30 A.M. to 4:30 P.M.; Saturday 10:00 A.M. to 4:00 P.M.; and Sunday 1:00 to 4:00 P.M. Call (301) 777–5905.

The romance of early twentieth-century steam railroading is with us once more on the **Allegany Central Railroad**, where passengers take a 17-mile ride combining mountaintop scenery and rich transportation history. The Allegany Central features two locomotives in the G5C class, one built in Montreal in 1946, the other in Kingston in 1948; both were used by the Canadian Pacific Railroad. Locomotive 1286 served in the Barbra Streisand film *Hello, Dolly*. Restoration of the locomotives has been accomplished with the help of rail enthusiasts from the eastern United States and Canada. The cars were built in the 1920s by Pullman for the Richmond, Fredericksburg, and Potomac railroads.

As the train steams its way up the 2.8 percent grade on the westward trip from Cumberland to Frostburg, it travels along old Western Maryland Railway and Cumberland and Pennsylvania Railway rights-of-way. Riders view many memorable sights including the famous Cumberland Narrows (a natural 1,000-foot breach in Will's Mountain known as the "Gateway to the West"), an iron truss bridge, Bone Cave, and Helmstetter's Horseshoe Curve.

You can drive to the top of either side of the Narrows for an unparalleled view of Cumberland and the surrounding countryside on a clear day. To reach the eastern wall of the Narrows, take Will's Mountain Road off Piedmont Avenue to the parking lot of Artmor Plastics, park, and walk about 2 blocks. To reach the western wall, take Exit 41, the Sacred Heart Hospital exit, off Route 40-48. Go through the traffic light and up the hill to Bishop Walsh Road where you will turn right to the high school. Drive to the back of the school, where the road ends, and walk through the woods, past the water tower, to the edge, about a five-minute walk. This is not a prepared path and is not handicapped accessible; it is not recommended for nighttime visits.

Other interesting sights along the way include the 1,000-foot Brush Mountain Tunnel, the Allegheny Front, Victorian architecture, the C & O Canal, Rocky Gap State Park, Green Ridge State Forest, Buck's Horse Farm, and the frontier town of Mt. Savage (where America's first iron rails were produced). At the Frostburg terminus you can get a close-up view of the engineer and fireman in blue-and-white overalls and the locomotive turntable, which reverses the train for the return journey.

At the other end, in Frostburg, James Oberhaus, Jr., has restored the **Old Depot Center** complex, which now features a restaurant, an ice-cream parlor, and a bakery. A special dining car has been dedicated as the Governor William Donald Schaefer Special for the governor who was credited with inspiring state, local, and private development of the scenic railroad. The trip takes about two and a half hours, including a one-hour layover in Frostburg. You can return by bus if you wish.

The train, operated by Jack Showalter, runs at 12:30 and 3:30 P.M. on weekends in May and September, and six days a week in June, July, and August. Additional trips are scheduled in October for fall foliage viewing. Tickets are $9.50 for

9

adults, $8.50 for senior citizens and students, and $5.00 for children from four through twelve. Children under four are free, and may be required to sit on your lap if the train is full.

Charter trips and special events such as dinner trips or trips featuring murder mysteries, dinner theater, or dancing are scheduled periodically. Private parties for weddings, birthdays, business meetings, school outings, and other events also may be booked. Write to Allegany Central Railroad, Western Maryland Station, Canal Street, Cumberland 21502, or call them at (800) TRAIN–50 or (301) 689–6668.

One of the sights you will see on the railroad excursion, or on a drive through Mt. Savage, is the **Mt. Savage Castle.** This National Historic Landmark in stone, built in 1874, is a replica of the Craig Castle in Scotland. At the height of its grandeur, the castle was owned by industrialist Andrew Ramsay, a Scot who was renowned for his production of ceramic glazed brick, which can be found throughout the building. He also planted the rare trees and abundant flowers that overflow the estate.

The castle's twenty-eight rooms, nine bathrooms, carriage house, and terraced gardens have been restored to their former elegance and furnished with antiques by William and Andrea Myer. The Myers now run the castle as a bed and breakfast with six elegantly furnished sleeping rooms. Four rooms have private baths; two rooms share a large main bathroom. A full breakfast is provided for overnight guests, and high tea is served between 3:00 and 4:00 p.m. Weather permitting, both are served in the outside courtyard or on the porticoes. In keeping with the Scottish tradition, croquet and putting can be enjoyed on the grassed terrace.

Rates range from $60 single occupancy for the Robert Burns Room, which has a four-poster, queen-sized bed, to $105 double occupancy for the Thistle Suite, which has double brass and trundle beds, sitting area, and full bath.

Tours, receptions, parties, conferences, and other special events may be booked at the Castle. Privacy is assured by a 20-foot stone wall that surrounds the grounds. The address is The Castle, Box 578, Mt. Savage 21545. Call (301) 759–5946.

Just as the railroad and the canal played an important part in the area's development, the National Pike has a claim to fame. A **National Pike Mural** was placed on the side of the

Fidelity Bank building in Frostburg in May 1989. The large, hand-painted mural, approximately 20 by 40 feet, was designed by local artist Philip Kenney. It depicts an early scene of the western approach to Frostburg, showing a covered wagon on the National Pike when it was a dirt toll road. It also depicts local coal mining. The Fidelity Bank is on East Main Street in Frostburg.

Westvaco Paper Company at Luke spreads over three counties and two states–Allegany and Garrett in Maryland and Mineral in West Virginia. The town is named for William Luke, who founded the paper company on this site in 1888. The company manufactures over 1,200 tons of high quality, coated, white printing papers each day. The products are used for such magazines as *Forbes*, *Town & Country*, *Good Housekeeping*, *Fortune*, and Disney and National Geographic Society publications.

A ninety-minute tour allows visitors to view the papermaking process from pulpwood to cooking to the finished rolls and sheets. Call (301) 359–3311 to arrange a tour. The company prefers about two weeks' notice.

When you are driving from the Oakland area of Garrett County to Luke, you will have several miles of a very steep downhill grade on Route 135 where trucks are cautioned to drive no more than 10 miles an hour. Assuming you are caught behind one of these trucks, slip into low gear (in the car and in your mind) and spend a little time looking at the beautiful countryside—something you would not be able to do if you were rushing through at fifty-five miles an hour. That is why you are off the beaten path, isn't it?

The **Lonaconing Iron Furnace** was erected about 1836 by the George's Creek Coal and Iron Company and produced iron for the next twenty years. When the furnace was constructed, it was unique in several respects. It was 50 feet high and 50 feet square at the base—a daring departure from contemporary furnaces, which were 30 feet high and 30 feet square. Moreover, it was the first furnace built in this country that successfully used coke fuel when all previous furnaces had used the less efficient charcoal.

The furnace was built against a hillside because it was fed from the top. The site was chosen because the necessary iron, ore, coal, wood, clay, limestone, sandstone, and water were

11

readily available, although transportation to the marketplace was not convenient. Castings made here included stoves, farming implements, and dowels for the C & O Canal lock walls.

Today the furnace is the backdrop for a pleasant town park in Lonaconing, where you can stop to lunch at the picnic tables or enjoy the play equipment. A sign notes the location of the former Central School, and a bronze plaque honors Robert Moses "Lefty" Grove, a native son who was elected into the Baseball Hall of Fame in 1947. Lauded as the greatest left-handed pitcher of all time, he played for the Philadelphia Athletics from 1925 to 1933 and the Boston Braves from 1934 to 1941. The furnace is located on Route 36, Main Street, in Lonaconing.

For additional information, write to Bev Bonarigo, Director, Allegany County Tourism and Public Relations, Western Maryland Station Center, Cumberland 21502, or call (301) 777-5905.

Garrett County

Garrett County claims several Maryland honors. It is the county farthest west, and it has the highest mountain (Backbone, at 3,360 feet), the tallest waterfall (Muddy Creek Falls, at 64 feet), and the largest lake (Deep Creek, with a length of 12 miles and a 69-mile shoreline).

Reportedly, it has the only town in the country named Accident. The story is that George Deakins was given a land grant for 600 acres in western Maryland in 1751 by King George II. Deakins sent two engineers on separate missions to find his paradise. By accident, each selected the same plot starting at the same tall oak tree. Deakins called this plot "The Accident Tract," and the name endures; locals wouldn't have it any other way. Most noted by visitors are the Accident Garage, the Accident Fire Department, and the Accident Professional Building.

The area was permanently settled by Colonel James McHenry (aide to General George Washington, signer of the Declaration of Independence, and the man for whom the Baltimore fort was named) around 1805. Vacationers have been seeking respite in Garrett County for decades, and

12

Lonaconing Iron Furnace

traces of that history can be found throughout the county. The Shawnee Indians summered here. People from the sunbaked, humid cities of Washington and Baltimore came here to enjoy the cool mountain climate as early as 1851. That is when the Baltimore and Ohio Railroad ran its line to Oakland, which would become the county seat. The train no longer stops in Garrett County, but the Oakland station, an outstanding and picturesque Queen Anne structure built in 1884, remains.

The Oakland Post Office Mural was created by Robert Gates in 1942; it portrays a buckwheat harvest. Gates also did the mural in the Bethesda Post Office, which depicts the Montgomery County Farm Woman's Cooperative Market.

Presidents Ulysses S. Grant, William Henry Harrison, and Grover Cleveland enjoyed this area as their vacation spot, and William McKinley stopped here while campaigning for office. Thomas Edison, Henry Ford, and Harvey Firestone camped by Muddy Creek Falls in 1918 and again in 1921. Even Albert Einstein is said to have spent two weeks here in 1946.

Grover Cleveland and his bride, Frances Folsom, stayed in the three-story, fourteen-room "Cottage Number Two," now "Cleveland Cottage," at the Deer Park Hotel for their fifteen-day wedding trip in 1886. The Deer Park Hotel was built in 1873 by the Baltimore and Ohio Railroad when John W. Garrett (for whom the county was named) was president. None of the hotel's main structure remains because it was razed in 1942, but some of the foundation is still visible. About 5 miles east of Oakland, on Route 135, turn south on Deer Park Hotel Road for ½ mile, then drive east on the loop at Pennington Cottage to reach the hotel.

Solomon Sterner opened the **Casselman Hotel** in Grantsville in 1824 to take in travelers from the National Pike. As usual with restaurants, inns, and hotels along the pike, this one is on the north side, or the side that westbound travelers would be on.

When the nearby **Casselman Bridge** was built in 1813, it was the largest single-span bridge in America. Gracefully curving 50 feet above the river, it was constructed so that the Chesapeake and Ohio Canal could travel beneath its span. The canal never came this far, but the bridge carried traffic for 125 years. It is closed to motorized traffic, but there's a picnic area and a scenic spot to enjoy for a few minutes or a few hours.

East of the Casselman Bridge is Penn-Alps, home to numerous crafters who work in log cabins that have been brought here from the surrounding countryside. The shops in the **Spruce Forest Artisan Village** are open from late May through late October. One of the better-known artists is a Grantsville native and resident, Gary Yoder. Yoder is a renowned bird carver who uses his chisels, knives, wood burners, and other tools to create birds that win prizes in international competition. In September of 1989 Yoder won a $20,000 prize for his robins at the Ward Foundation world championships in Ocean City, Maryland.

Yoder has been carving for twenty of his thirty-one years, and his carvings can sell from $300 to more than $10,000. Orders can take from two to four years to fill. When you visit Yoder's bird-carving cabin, he will be delighted to explain how birds are carved. He may test your visual acuity by asking you to distinguish between his carved bird feather and a real bird feather. Other crafts are sold in the gift shop.

Penn Alps is on Alternate Route 40, Grantsville. Their phone number is (301) 895–5985.

About a mile east of Grantsville, still on the National Pike, is the **Fuller-Baker Log House**. The house is representative of those constructed on the Allegheny frontier, except that it is large enough to have been a tavern. It is believed to be the only remaining log tavern on the National Pike between Cumberland and Wheeling. Maryland's first governor, Thomas Johnson, owned the property when the house was built in 1815, but it is named for two other longtime residents. The first was Henry Fuller, who came to the area in 1837 to work as a stonemason. The Bakers were also early settlers and owned the house at a later date. The house is now on the National Register.

Woodcarver Dennis Ruane is restoring it for use as a studio. Ruane was one of the demonstrators at Penn Alps after he moved here in 1984; today you can see his work, which is a mix of large and small items, such as spoons and Christmas tree ornaments, when you stop by the log house. Contact Ruane at P.O. Route 1, Grantsville 21536 or call (301) 895–3172.

In 1925 a dam, 1,300 feet long and 62 feet high, was constructed to provide hydroelectric power, and **Deep Creek Lake** resulted. It is fed by Deep and Cherry creeks, seven stream runs, and two glades. Rafters on the Upper Youghiogheny River (or Upper Yough, pronounced "yuck") fight their way over Gap and Bastard falls and through rapids with names like Charlie's Choice, Rocky III, Cheeseburger, and Meat Cleaver.

In the 9-mile ride there are twenty class IV and V rapids (the top of the scale being class VI) and a downhill drop of 100 to 120 feet per mile. These rapids can provide some tough but exhilarating times; an experienced guide is a necessity.

When the Whitewater Canoe/Kayak World Championships were held in the United States for the first time in 1989, they were held on the nearby Savage River, another popular rafting place.

Other recreational pastimes in Garrett County include water sports, skiing (downhill and cross country), hiking, camping, golfing, horseback riding, hunting, and tennis. The mountains in this area receive the second largest annual snowfall in the east (after the White Mountains of New Hampshire), which makes for good downhill skiing at Wisp (Deep Creek Lake) and extraordinary cross-country skiing.

River and Trail Outfitters teach cross-country skiing and conduct trips every weekend from late January to mid-March. A weekend session includes ski lessons and trail skiing through New Germany State Park, equipment rental, five country-style meals with home-baked breads and pies, a Saturday evening wine and cheese party, and a room for two nights at the Casselman Inn. Prices are about $200 per person, with family rates available. A day trip is $60 per person and includes instruction, trail skiing, ski rentals, and a hot lunch. For additional information write to River and Trail Outfitters, 604 Valley Road, Knoxville 21758, or call (301) 695–5177.

The climate, people, and recreational offerings in the area combined to attract Gordon K. "Sandy" Douglas about thirty years ago when he started building his Flying Scot sailboat at the **Gordon Douglas Boat Company.** Eric and Mary Ammann have been supervising the operation for the past few years, overseeing the construction of these handmade boats, which come out of the plant at the rate of about two a week.

The Ammanns have maintained the image and reputation of the hugely popular Flying Scot. This fast 19-footer has a wide beam and a large center cockpit. It also features a fiberglass centerboard instead of a keel. It can be sailed by one, but it will carry eight people comfortably on a day's sail. A novice supposedly can learn the basics in six hours. If you like to look at sailboats, you can tour the plant at Deer Park between 10:00 A.M. and 4:00 P.M. weekdays. Call (301) 334–4848.

About 20 miles east of Oakland is the Baltimore and Ohio Viaduct at Bloomington. It was opened in 1851 to connect the port of Baltimore with industrial Wheeling and the Ohio Valley. The multispan, stone and concrete bridge carries the railroad across the North Branch of the Potomac River. A confederate raiding party schemed to demolish the viaduct but was driven away by Union troops before the bridge could be blasted. Blasting holes drilled by Captain John H. McNeill and his McNeill's Rangers are still visible on the bridge. The Baltimore and Ohio Viaduct is on Route 135, just west of the Garrett and Allegany county line.

Garrett has one other "first" honor. In 1989, Frank "Doc" Custer sent 3,200 of his white pine and balsam fir Christmas trees to the Bahamas. This was the first time that a Maryland grower had exported trees outside the United States. Custer planted his first tree in 1956, and his Mountain Top Tree Farm, outside of Oakland, is one of the largest tree growers in the state. As you drive around the county and spot the perfect tree for your next holiday season, remember it may be going to Nassau to brighten up someone's holiday who misses snow and cold weather.

For additional information contact the Deep Creek Lake—Garrett County Promotion Council, Garrett County Courthouse, Oakland 21550, or call (301) 334–1948. Diane Wolfe is the Executive Director there.

Washington County

Washington County—the first county to be named after George Washington—was founded on September 6, 1776, just days after our country itself. In a Civil War battle fought at Sharpsburg, along Antietam Creek, more than 23,000 casualties were suffered, making it the bloodiest confrontation in our history.

Starting in 1989, an annual remembrance of this day is held in mid-December, signified by 23,110 luminaries placed every 10 feet along 4½ miles of roadway, in the fields, in Bloody Lane, and around some of the monuments. It takes 400 volunteers to set the lights, starting at 3:30 P.M. About 3,000 cars drive through to look at the candles, starting about 5:30 P.M.; the candles burn about ten hours. The luminaries are paid for by corporate sponsors, and the drive is free, but a donation is requested.

The idea came from the Rest Haven cemetery, which had previously placed a luminary at every gravesite. Borrowing the idea, Hagerstown residents lit luminaries every night for the two weeks prior to Christmas. One night it was the north side of town, another it was the south side, and so it continued throughout the area. Band members of the high schools sold 81,000 lights in the neighborhoods.

Washington County parks rate with the best, including the C & O Canal National Historical Park, the Appalachian Trail (37 miles), Fort Frederick State Park, Washington Monument State Park, Pen Mar County Park (and at least eight other county parks), and Hagerstown City Park.

Hagerstown, the county seat of Washington County, is also the home of the *Hagers-Town Town and Country Almanack*, which has been printed since 1797. The weather forecasts generate the most interest, and people swear by it. In fact, there is a folk tale that the book called for snow on July 4, 1874, and that it did snow on that date. Research indicates that the almanac did not predict snow, and the minimum temperature for that day was said to have been in the high sixties—not too conducive to snow.

You might wonder, without being arrogant, how people live so far out in the country. You think about snow blocking roads for days and people being miles from a store or a neighbor. Where do these people work? What do they do for a living?

One set of answers can be found in the members of the **Valley Craft Network.** This group of nine artisans, most of whom are in Washington County, spend their days creating works of art and their weekends traveling around the country-side visiting craft shows. Twice a year, in March or April and on the first weekend in December, they sponsor a Studio Tour. Many people make a weekend visit out of the studio tour.

A map and STUDIO TOUR signs help you to negotiate the back roads of Pleasant Valley between Hagerstown, Frederick, and Harper's Ferry, so you completely forget you're barely an hour from Washington or Baltimore. A side benefit of the winter tour is that every studio has a steaming pot of apple cider and something to nibble on waiting to warm you up on a nippy day.

Each crafter has a catalog or some type of brochure from which you can order. You can visit most of them any time of the year, with the normal precaution of calling ahead to make sure someone will be there. There are many other crafters throughout the valley who are worthy of your atten-tion besides the members of the Valley Craft Network. You will see advertising signs along the roadway or brochures in shops to let you know where they are. The following list includes only Network members and is just a sampling of the many local crafts you can enjoy.

Bud and Rachel Janse of the Dreaming Deer travel each spring or summer to the wilds of Wyoming, Montana, Idaho, and Colorado in search of deer, moose, or elk antlers that were shed over the year so that they can create next year's pipes, earrings, necklaces, bola ties, and other antler items. The rest of the year you can find them in a Victorian chapel at 103 West Main Street, Burkittsville 21718 (301–834–8476 or –6490).

Also in Burkittsville is Deva Natural Clothing. John and Nancy Coker and Martin Paule sell handcrafted natural fiber clothing for men and women in a luscious array of tones and textures. They promise to get you out of your jeans, and as comfortable as these clothes are, they'll probably get their way.

As the owners say, "Deva is an eleven-year-old experiment

19

committed to redefining the wardrobe and the workplace."
Their comfortable, loose-fitting cotton clothing includes bib
overalls and tops that need no fasteners. A network of more
than fifty friends and neighbors work at home, handcrafting
clothes that are free from the dictates of fashion.

Their family approach is evident during nice weather when
Deva workers, children, dogs, and guests like you get togeth-
er for lunch and volleyball. Visitors are welcome from 8:00
A.M. until 5:00 P.M. weekdays and 10:00 A.M. until 4:00 P.M. on
Saturday. The address is Deva Natural Clothing, 303 East
Main Street, Burkittsville 21718 (301–663–4900).

Holly Prothro creates soft-sculpture designs and specializes in animals, such as an owl or tortoise. Hunt Prothro
makes stoneware with interesting swirl patterns as well as
framed tile paintings, sculptured porcelain wall reliefs and
murals, and large decorative platters. Contact Prothro
Designs at P.O. Box 114, Rohrersville 21756 (301–432–5739).

Eric Madsen is another potter who creates functional
stoneware in a restored barn at Chance Regained Farm. The
address is Eric Madsen Pottery, Park Hall Road, Rohrersville
21779 (301–432–2874).

Del Martin is known for his wheel-thrown tableware,
lamps, sinks, and planters; he is located at Foxcross Pottery,
6640 Remsburg Road, Sharpsburg 21782 (301–432–6692).

Nancy Walz creates herb and everlasting wreaths and bou-
quets and also sells hand-dipped candles in her restored
summer kitchen at Surreybrooke, 8537 Hollow Road,
Middletown 21769 (301–371–7466).

Michelle Reilly offers a kaleidoscope of quilts, fabrics, and
handspun yarns and fleece straight from the sheep. A large
Bernese Mountain Dog, named Yankee, waits to greet you
and expects a lot of love and petting. The address is Wool 'N'
Quilts, 4614 Locust Grove Road, Rohrersville 21779 (301–
432–2009).

Jan Richardson and her Windy Meadows Pottery is perhaps
the best known crafter in the valley; her hand-built stoneware
houses can be seen everywhere. From a little privy (a night
light for your modern privy) to a chapel, from a train depot to
an ice-cream parlor, you can find the perfect representation
of yesterday's small town. Some items are created in limited
editions and have become valued collector's items.

If you travel at times other than the Studio Tour, you can visit the Windy Meadows operation to see how clay is readied for the various crafters who hand assemble the stoneware houses in their homes. Periodically, Jan issues a newsletter and photo brochure, which includes her schedule of craft shows. Windy Meadows is located at 1036 Valley Road, Knoxville 21758 (301–663–4115; 834–8857; 432–6231).

Another of the members is the Catoctin Pottery, which is located in Jefferson, in Frederick County. While you are here or at any of the other studios you can ask for a list of nearby restaurants and other attractions.

A favorite of ours is the **Beaver Creek House Bed and Breakfast,** operated by Don and Shirley Day. The home was built in 1905 and the rooms are filled with family antiques and memorabilia. The white brick home with dark shutters is huge, yet warm and friendly with a great wraparound porch where you can sit on a swing and watch the scenery go by. Particularly pleasing are sunrises over the Blue Ridge mountains, should you be up that early. Guests in any of the seven rooms may have breakfast on the screen porch, in the courtyard, or in the dining room, and share afternoon tea in the parlor.

Weekend rates are $70 double and $60 single; deduct $10 for weeknights. Route 1, Box 330, Hagerstown 21740 (301–797–4764).

For lodgings with a real twist, you'll want to visit the **Maple Tree Campground** near Gathland State Park. The unusual feature of this campground is that you sleep in a tree house. Did you always want one when you were a kid, but you lived in the city, or the only adults around had sixteen thumbs? This is not quite as rustic as you might remember, but it is as close as most of us will ever get. Your tree house—on stilts about 7 feet off the ground—has a couple of bunks (bring a sleeping bag), a wood stove, a table with benches, and a filled woodbin. A communal bathhouse is nearby, you have twenty-six acres of woods to roam and explore, and you're not far from the Appalachian Trail. You may bring your tent for "regular" camping.

Pets, on leash at all times, are welcome. Reservations are recommended. Rates run about $30 per night for up to four people for a tree cottage, $20 per night for a standard tree house, $4 per person per night for standard tent sites, and $3 for primitive tent sites.

When Phyllis Sorocko started this campground after retirement, she dreaded the idea of tearing up the land and trees for campsites and dumpsites and was thrilled with this compromise. The campground is located on Townsend Road, Gapland 21736. Call (301) 432–5585.

The Washington County Museum of Fine Art is an outstanding museum overlooking the fifty-acre City Park Lake (home to 200 waterfowl, including black swans). It was the idea and gift of Mr. and Mrs. William Henry Singer, Jr., who had collected numerous possessions during their European travels and were looking for a beautiful place to house them. The cornerstone was laid on July 15, 1930 by Mrs. Singer's grandniece, Anna Spencer Brugh.

The museum was built of homewood brick with Indiana limestone trim. Two wings were added in 1949: the Memorial Gallery, in honor of Mr. Singer, who died in 1943, and the Concert Gallery, in honor of Mrs. Singer's love of music. Mrs. Singer was eighty-six when she died in Laren, Holland, in 1962.

Among the museum's collection are the works of Mr. Singer, who was a post-impressionist painter of note. Many of his landscapes show the fishing villages, fjords, and snow-covered mountains of Norway, where the Singers lived. Also in the collection are Old Masters, twentieth-century sculpture and painting, and a variety of decorative arts from around the world. The emphasis, though, is on American art.

The twentieth-century American artist William Glackens is now represented through a gift of Mr. and Mrs. Ira Glackens of Shepherdstown, West Virginia, who donated his floral still life entitled "Bouquet in Blue Paper-Wrapped Pot." Glackens was a member of "The Eight," a group of American artists who promoted realism in art through their works on canvas. With this addition, the museum has works by six of "The Eight," including Glackens, Arthur Bowen Davies, Robert Henri, Ernest Lawson, George B. Luks, and John Sloan.

In addition to tours, the museum offers art classes (weaving, clay, acrylics, quilting, and more), lectures, films, and music recitals. A bimonthly calendar is available.

The museum, located on City Park Lake, is open Tuesday through Saturday from 10:00 A.M. to 5:00 P.M. and Sunday from 1:00 to 6:00 p.m. A donation is requested. Call (301) 739–5727.

Hagerstown has a history of railroading, and you can see it portrayed at the Model Railroad Museum, now located at the Fairgrounds. You have to navigate three flights of rickety steps to a large room to see this display of local railroading.

Three **Hagerstown Post Office Murals** represent different aspects of the railway transportation of mail. The paintings were done by Frank Long of Berea, Kentucky, as part of the Section of Fine Arts program—placing appropriate art in federal buildings. They were done in 1938. The first painting depicts mailbags being loaded onto a train. A central panel depicts a railway post office in operation, with postal clerks sorting letters on a train. The third panel over the lockboxes shows figures on the station platform watching an approaching train that will pick up the mail. Frank Long also painted post office murals in Louisville and Berea, Kentucky; Crawfordsville, Indiana; and Drumright, Oklahoma.

Boonsboro is known for its Civil War museum, but those who really know it, know to visit in August and September when Boonsboro cantaloupes ripen. You can buy them from a roadside stand, particularly on Saturdays and Sundays, but it's best to plan an outing and pick your own. Then you'll really enjoy the thin-skinned, "Heart of Gold" variety with all its natural sweetness.

The **Wilson Village Old General Store** is a classic country store with a post office, penny candy, yard goods, and much more. You'll also see a one-room schoolhouse. The store is on Old Route 40, and it is open daily. Call (301) 582–0640.

On your way to Wilson Village from Hagerstown, you may stop by the **Historic Wilson Bridge Picnic Area.** It's located along Route 40 West, adjacent to Historic Wilson Bridge, which is the oldest, longest, and most graceful of twenty-three stone arch bridges in the country. The five-arch span was built in 1819 as an early extension of the National Pike to the Ohio Valley. The structure was erected by Pennsylvanian Silas Harry at a cost of $12,000. Its style represented a triumph for the justices of the Levy Court (until 1829, the

23

Wilson Village Old General Store

1829, the body similar to a Board of County Commissioners) who insisted on an all-stone structure in the face of army engineers' arguments that a wooden bridge laid over stone piers would suffice.

The bridge is about 200 feet north of the west end of the "new" bridge crossing the Conococheague, 5 miles west of Hagerstown on Route 40. This one-acre site offers picnic tables, parking, and canoe access to the Conococheague Creek.

Of particular interest to sports fans is the Hagerstown Suns baseball team of the Eastern League. This AA team draws more than 160,000 fans a year; it is a farm club of the Baltimore Orioles. In previous years, loyalists have seen the likes of Jeff Ballard, Jim Palmer, Bill Ripkin, and Craig Worthington, all of whom have gone on to be well known in the baseball world. Palmer was elected to the Baseball Hall of Fame in 1989, his first year of eligibility. For information call the Municipal Stadium at (301) 791–6266.

The Washington County Tourism office has a number of interesting brochures, and the personnel there are delighted to help you. Those traveling with children, or those who are young at heart, will love the Kid's Stuff brochure listing one hundred things to do, from the Mt. Briar Wetlands Preserve to the ghost walk at Fort Frederick at Halloween time.

In the *Off the Beaten Path* series, we like to find fine dining in unusual and unexpected places. Hancock's **Park-N-Dine** restaurant, overlooking the C & O Canal, is not fine in a culinary sense, but it is extraordinary. The Burnett family opened it August 2, 1946, and it has been growing in size and reputation since then (with a major addition about every five years; at last count the place could seat 210 people). The interior has plain, bare tables; pictures of the 1940 Hancock High School graduation class and the twenty-two members of the 1925 class; artificial flowers; Melmac dishes; and plenty of hard-working people. The view of the canal and the Potomac River are terrific and perhaps are best from the Blue Room.

However, the view isn't the main reason that 5,000 to 6,000 people come here every week and that 25 percent of the diners are locals. It's because you can still get an all-you-can-eat meal for as low as $3. Says Roger Burnett, "I always tell them in the kitchen to put as much on the plate as they can get on." They do. And the plate is pastel plastic with little divider sections. Almost every dish comes with a huge serving of stuffing. Each week Park-N-Dine goes through a thousand pounds of ham, turkey, and roast beef, as well as two tons of potatoes. We doubt if anyone knows how many tons of stuffing are served. You can count the desserts served on one hand, because no one has room for anything after the meal.

The view of the C & O Canal draws nearly as many people as the food. Hundreds of people stop by for Sunday dinner, and at last inspection the restaurant was being enlarged again. Park-N-Dine is open Monday through Saturday from 6:00 A.M. to 10:00 P.M. and Sunday from 7:00 A.M. to 10:00 P.M. Mother's Day is the busiest. It was open twenty-four hours a day for thirty-five years, but that stopped a few years back. The address is 189 East Main Street, Hancock 21750. Call (301) 678–5242.

Seven miles west of Hancock, near the border between Allegany and Washington counties is **Sideling Hill.** A new freeway, officially designated Highway 48, diverts traffic off a steep, tricky road that twists to a roundhouse curve at the top of Sideling Hill. The 4.5-mile section of the road took twenty-eight months to complete and cost about twenty-one million dollars. Workers blasted an incredible, breath-taking 360-foot-deep cut in the mountain, which reveal millions of years of geological history; all this to achieve a relatively flat roadway. A three-and-a-half story, handicapped-accessible interpretive center, which is approachable from both sides of the highway, will let you see all those layers and folds of multihued rocks that have been exposed by the cut and will explain their geologic history.

For additional tourism information, write to Robert O'Connor, Washington County Tourism Division, 1826-C Dual Highway, Hagerstown 21740. Call (301) 791–3130 or 797–8800, a twenty-four–hour information number.

Off the Beaten Path in Central Maryland

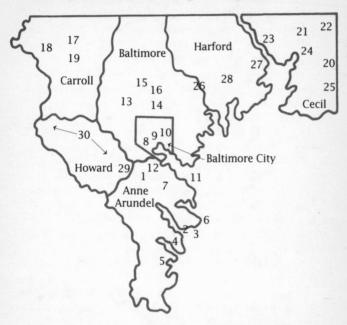

1. Baltimore-Washington International (BWI) Airport
2. Banneker-Douglass Museum of Afro-American Life and History
3. U.S. Naval Academy Museum
4. Adam's, the Place for Ribs
5. The Bread Place
6. Sandy Point State Park
7. British Brewing Company
8. Top of the World Trade Center
9. Maryland Viet Nam Veterans Memorial
10. Painted screens
11. General Motors Baltimore Assembly Plant
12. Calvert Distilling Company
13. Wild Acres Trail
14. Asian Arts Center
15. Oregon Ridge Park and Nature Center
16. Ashland Furnace
17. Hashawha Environmental Appreciation Center
18. Bicycle tours
19. Ghosts of Carroll County
20. Little Wedding Chapel
21. Covered bridges
22. Fair Hill Inn
23. Conowingo Hydroelectric Plant
24. Day Basket Factory
25. Schaefer's Canal House
26. Jerusalem Covered Bridge
27. Susquehanna Trading Company
28. Liriodendron
29. Thomas Viaduct
30. Cider Mill Farm and Larriland Farms

Central Maryland

Perhaps nowhere in the state is there more diversity than in the area referred to as Central Maryland. In the rolling foothills and picturesque landscapes of this region are horse farms and vineyards, the commercial center of Baltimore city, huge stone farmhouses and old mills, busy waterways surrounding the Chesapeake Bay and its tributaries, some of the oldest towns in the country, and modern, vibrant cities. This core of six counties and two major cities encompasses it all.

This is the area that almost every travel writer writes about. In keeping with our "off the beaten path" dictum, we have looked for the unusual even in that which is familiar.

Sixteen million vehicles use the William Preston Lane, Jr., or Chesapeake Bay, Bridge every year. Only 50,000 people walk across it, though, on Chesapeake Bay Bridge Walk Day. Once Maryland was a leading contender in the number of "kissing" or covered bridges; now there are only a few. We sought out the ones in this region and even located one that is on private property (see also Frederick and Prince George's counties in the Greater Washington section).

Countless people stop by Annapolis to see its waterfront, Ego Alley (where the expensive boats parade), and the United States Naval Academy. They watch the sailboats in harbor—even in the winter, when there is a Frostbite series—or the Naval Academy's noon meal formation, when the brigade of midshipmen, attired in their dress uniforms, assembles in front of Bancroft Hall for inspection. We chatted with Robert F. Sumrall, who recreates scale models of the ships that have plied the Bay.

Whenever anyone talks about the Chesapeake Bay, blue crabs and oysters are sure to be discussed. We include a distinguished delicatessen, a bakery, an admirable place for ribs, a German restaurant that can compare with many fine art galleries, an old inn that is relatively new, and a scenic waterside eatery for sightseeing while you dine.

In a city as vibrant as Baltimore ("If you haven't seen Baltimore in five years, then you haven't seen Baltimore"), we chose to focus on the traditional: white marble steps and window screen painters.

We want you to do all the "touristy" things—spend an evening at the Morris Mechanic Theatre at Hopkins Plaza, eat crabs until you are elbow-deep in shells and seasonings at Harborplace, catch the superlative Walters Art Gallery—but we hope you will take time to visit some of our favorite "off the beaten path" places, too.

Anne Arundel County

Millions of people each year pass through the **Baltimore-Washington International Airport (BWI)** to catch a plane, to pick up a passenger or to go home. They do not realize that the airport has more to offer them. The airport is open and airy, and in Concourse B is a stained-glass sculpture of that Maryland delicacy, the blue crab.

Created by Jackie Leatherbury Douglass and John Douglass, the crab is made of white glass from West Germany and other colors of Blenko glass from West Virginia. This sculpture is 5 feet high, 10 feet wide, and 7 feet deep and weights about 400 pounds. Jackie also has a piece in the Smithsonian Institution's Air and Space Museum in Washington, D.C. For additional information about their artwork, which includes illustrations for books about shells and fishes, write to Parish Creek Artists, P.O. Box 56, Shady Side 20764, or call (301) 261–5599 or 867–2222.

A shuttle bus connects the airport to the nearby Amtrak station, and limousine (van and bus) service provides door-to-door transportation to and from the airport.

Walking tours of the airport are provided through Joseph T. Herbert of the marketing office for groups of twelve to thirty people, with a minimum age of nine. Usually, these are school children or civic organizations, VIP groups, or special-interest groups, such as firefighters or engineers, who receive a "behind the scenes" tour. Individuals who want an airport tour may call to see if a group tour is scheduled that they could join. The normal tour includes visits to and explanations of the baggage claim area, airline ticket counters, restaurants, gift shops, gate departure areas, the National Weather Service, and all the major concourses. Call at least a week to ten days ahead for group tours; the telephone is (301) 261–1000 from the Washington, D.C., area, or (301) 859–7034 from elsewhere.

When airport construction was started on May 4, 1947, the airport site was known as Friendship, and many old homes and farms on the 3,200-acre tract were demolished. Only Rezin Howard Hammond's home was left standing, where it remains today at the edge of the airport. Originally known as Cedar Farm because of the cedar trees on the property, it was built in 1820 from bricks made of clay dug on the farm.

It is now the Benson-Hammond House and is used by the Ann Arrundell County Historical Society, whose purpose is to encourage the appreciation among the general public of "the smaller centers of culture where so much of our heritage lies hidden."

Within the house are a collection of dolls, a display of tokens known as picker checks (made of aluminum, fiberboard, and brass stamped into various shapes and used as currency by farmers, each of whom had his own set of checks with his initials), a miniature replica of Angel's Store in Pasadena, and a growing library of historical and genealogical materials on the second floor. The museum is open for tours on special occasions, and the library is open on Thursday from 10:00 A.M. to 3:00 P.M. A user's fee of $1 per day is charged for non-members.

The Browse and Buy Shoppe is also located at the house; it is open for the same Thursday hours and other times as volunteers are available. Call the Benson-Hammond House (Hammonds Ferry Road and Poplar Avenue, Linthicum) at (301) 768–9518 for tours and additional information.

A second Browse and Buy Shoppe is located at the Jones Station, at the corner of Old Annapolis and Jones Station roads. This late nineteenth-century building was one of the "step-down transformer" power stations for one of the two railroads serving Annapolis. There are no railroads performing that function these days; reportedly, Annapolis is the only state capital without such service. Hours at the Browse and Buy Shoppe are Tuesday through Saturday, 10:00 A.M. to 3:00 P.M.; call (301) 544–3370.

Visitors to Annapolis have a treat in store for them. Annapolis is authentic colonial architecture; Colonial Williamsburg in Virginia had to recreate that which is already here. Annapolis is called a "museum without walls" because of the dozens of eighteenth-century buildings in the city, but Annapolitans are quick to point out that it is a living museum, not an artificial one.

Annapolis is old-world charm, the United States Naval Academy, sailboats and powerboats by the hundreds (168,000 boats were registered in Maryland in 1984), antique shops, taverns, and, most of all, narrow, winding, hilly cobblestone streets that invite walking and exploring.

The Banneker-Douglass Museum of Afro-American Life and History is installed in a handsome Victorian-Gothic structure that was the Mount Moriah African Methodist Episcopal Church. The church served the community from 1874 until 1971. The museum is named for Benjamin Banneker (mathematician, scientist, astronomer, and surveyor) and Frederick Douglass (writer, journalist, civil libertarian, abolitionist, and U.S. minister and consul general to Haiti), both of whom were born and lived in Maryland. Banneker was appointed to serve on a commission that surveyed and laid out the capital. He had such a phenomenal memory that he produced, in detail, Pierre L'Enfant's plans for the District of Columbia when L'Enfant left—with the plans—before the job was finished.

Permanent and rotating displays are found in the Hall of National Greatness, the Gallery of Black Maritime History, the Herbert M. Frisby Hall (Frisby was a Baltimore science educator, war correspondent for Afro-American newspapers, and explorer who made twenty-one trips to the Arctic region and was the second black explorer to reach the North Pole), and the reference library. The museum features Afro-American arts and crafts, lectures, and films, all to encourage a better understanding of the contributions of Afro-Americans to Maryland and our country. Today's legacy is represented by prominent black artists, such as Josephine Gross, Gerald Hawkes, Laurence Hurst, and Hughie Lee-Smith, whose works adorn the walls of the gallery.

The Banneker-Douglass Museum is located at 84 Franklin Street, Annapolis. Hours are Tuesday through Friday, 10:00 A.M. to 3:00 P.M. and Saturday 12:00 noon to 4:00 P.M.; call

(301) 974–2893 for information.

In July 1989, some fifteen small, brittle bones, carefully wrapped in yellowed paper, were gently placed in a golden urn and laid to rest in a shady cemetery plot near St. Mary's Church in Annapolis. In mid-1987 the Reverend John Murray of St. Mary's had found these remains of St. Justin, who was beheaded at the age of twenty-six in the second century A.D.

According to Murray, it is not unusual for churches in Europe to have special tombs containing the relics of saints or martyrs, but few churches in the United States can claim such items because the country is so young. St. Justin's remains arrived in Baltimore in 1873 so the Reverend Joseph Wissel could protect them while Italy was in the middle of a political upheaval. Reverend Wissel and those who followed him displayed them prominently, but during the 1960s the church was renovated and the remains were placed in a box in a church safe.

The St. Mary's Church gardens are open to the public periodically during the year; the dates are advertised in the local newspapers. Call Dr. Robert Worden in the evening for additional information (301–263–0744).

One of the most fascinating exhibits is the display of model ships at the **U.S. Naval Academy Museum,** which features the work of Henry Huddleston Rogers and Robert F. Sumrall, an extraordinary model builder. Sumrall is the curator charged with repairing and maintaining a fleet of 225 little ships, some of them more than 300 years old. Sumrall built his first model when he was six and went on to be a naval architect, author, historian, model builder, and one of the most highly regarded authorities on ship models and model construction.

Sumrall has built models of significant and famous Maryland ships, including the *Dolphin*, the *Pride of Baltimore*, the *J. T. Leonard* (a unique oyster dredger), and the skipjack *Minnie V.* Most of the work Sumrall does for the Academy museum is in the realm of repair, maintenance, and restoration. His creative work, such as the commission for a 6-foot-tall model of the skipjack *Stanley Norman* (the original of which still operates on the Chesapeake) for the Occidental Restaurant in Washington, D.C., he does at home. He also has done an interpretive model of the *Arizona* wreck for the National

Park Service memorial at Pearl Harbor, and he is doing another of the Japanese flagship, *Akagi.* Private collections hold his battleship *Wisconsin* and several destroyers, which are located in Coronado, Virginia Beach, New York, and a gallery in Old Town Alexandria.

The Naval Academy Museum provides a valuable and convenient reference source for studying naval history. The museum is open 9:00 A.M. to 5:00 P.M. Monday through Saturday and 11:00 A.M. to 5:00 P.M. on Sunday. Contact them at (301) 267–2109 or 267–2108.

The skipjack is the symbol of the Chesapeake Bay waterman. These boats were developed in the 1890s, and they are the last surviving commercial sailing fleet in the United States. The oyster-dredging boats have become an endangered species, as their number has dwindled from about 1,500 at the turn of the century to about eighty on the water in 1958 and about three dozen in working condition now.

Annapolis has always been a vital area for commerce and trade, particularly when it comes to importing and exporting goods. But one of its most unusual commercial roles happened in 1862, when it became the major depot in the East for holding exchanged prisoners of war. Prisoners were held here until their back pay (earned during their incarceration) could be given to them.

At first they were camped at St. John's College, but the eight small, wooden barracks were inadequate for groups as large as 6,000 men at one time. Two hundred and fifty acres of farmland outside of Annapolis were rented from Charles S. and Ann Rebecca Welch for $125 per month. The forty-four barracks and all other buildings were sold at auction some time after 1865, when all the prisoners had been released. All that remains of this mustering place for Union prisoners, called Camp Parole, is the name of the town, Parole, on the western side of Annapolis.

Of special allure are the Historic Inns of Annapolis, each casting its captivating spell for those who want to sense history while enjoying the pleasures of modern accommodations. Even the names—Governor Calvert House, Robert Johnson House, Reynolds Tavern, State House Inn, and Maryland Inn—conjure up thoughts of legendary times and days of heroic deeds.

33

We have particularly fond memories of the Maryland Inn at Church Circle. It was constructed by Thomas Hyde in 1772 and has operated continuously as an inn since the late eighteenth century. The inn sits on a triangular lot called the "drummer's lot," the area where the town drummer, or crier, told of the day's news in the early eighteenth century. For years the King of France Tavern in the Maryland Inn's cellar has been the best home for live entertainment around. Ethen Ennis, Charlie Byrd, Tim Eyermann, and others have filled its brick-walled room with delightful sounds and good times. In years past, the Maryland Inn was where some of the Maryland legislators met each night after the day's session was over to discuss legislative business.

For information about the inns you can write to Historic Inns of Annapolis, 7 Church Circle, Annapolis 21401, or call (301) 263–6599; their toll-free numbers are (800) 638–8902 (in Maryland) and (800) 847–8882 (outside the state).

"Adam's, the Place for Ribs" is the claim of this Edgewater restaurant, and we agree with this bit of immodesty. In a couple of plain rooms with bare tables and a little bit of history on the walls, you will enjoy delicious barbecued baby back ribs, chicken, pork, and minced beef brisket, with the traditional side orders of coleslaw and fries. The menu is simple, and the carryout menu is even simpler; the next party at your house could feature coleslaw or beef or pork barbecue from Adam's.

The restaurant is at 169 Mayo Road, Edgewater; call (301) 956–2995 or 798–5170. It is open Monday through Friday from 4:00 to 11:00 P.M. and Saturday and Sunday from 1:00 to 11:00 P.M.

There are bakeries and then there are bakeries, and **The Bread Place** is one of those small, extraordinary ones. Richard Savel opened this bakery in the early 1980s, and it has been a sensation ever since. Saturday and Sunday mornings seem more cheerful after a few minutes in this delicious-smelling shop. Whether it is a meeting, a wedding, or a need for donuts or holiday treats, much of the population of this area seems to gravitate here. The fare includes contemporary cakes, European pastries, Danish cookie platters, hearth breads, hors d'oeuvres, roasted meats, salads, and sandwich platters. The Bread Place is open and baking seven days a week at 1308 Forest Drive, Annapolis 21403 (301–268–6677).

An unofficial declaration of spring's arrival is the annual Chesapeake Bay Bridge Walk Day. The walk was first held in 1975 after a Towson, Maryland scout leader noticed that one span was closed for construction and suggested one span could be closed for a day-long walk. An estimated 50,000 pedestrians as well as people in wheelchairs and on crutches cross the eastbound lanes of the bridge, and the only automobiles and trucks permitted belong to official vehicles and media trucks. Jogging, running, skateboards, bikers, and pets (except seeing-eye dogs) are prohibited; an early-morning race has been established for those who want to speed across the bridge instead of spending about ninety minutes walking the bridge and investigating various expansion joints, girder construction, architectural design, and engineering and assembly facets.

Pedestrians normally are not allowed on the 4.3-mile structure connecting the Annapolis area to the large spit of land known as the Eastern Shore. Blue waters lap innocuously about 185 feet below the twin spans of the bridge, also known as the William Preston Lane, Jr., Memorial Bridge.

Parking lots in Annapolis and at Anne Arundel Community College and also on the Eastern Shore start filling at 8:00 A.M. Buses start taking walkers over to the east side at 9:00 A.M. There is no charge for parking, the bus trip, or the walk.

Following the walk, participants are shuttled to the adjacent **Sandy Point State Park** for a celebration of the Bay. A variety of entertainment is scheduled, and information about the Bay is available. Sandy Point is the site of an award-winning accessible playground that is particularly challenging and rewarding to those with physical and mental impairments. The Maryland Forest, Park and Wildlife Service (MFPWS) has been busy addressing the issue of accessibility on two fronts. The first is the removal of architectural barriers to access, and the second is the development of programs that can be enjoyed by everyone, including those with impaired mobility, sight, or hearing.

Most likely the newest museum in Maryland is the Captain Salem Avery House in Shady Side, which opened its doors in mid-September of 1989. Avery's home was built in 1860 on the banks of the West River and was purchased by the Shady Side Rural Heritage Society to establish a museum to "protect, document, and illustrate the history and traditions" of Shady Side. The Society is particularly pleased that they were able to obtain some of the original Avery furniture from the owners of the house. The Captain Avery House is located at 1418 East West Shady Side Road, Shady Side 20764. The house is open by appointment, call T. C. Magnotti at (301) 261–9223 or LaVerne Papian at (301) 261–9384.

In April 1988 Craig Stuart-Paul and Rebecca Burk opened the **British Brewing Company** in Glen Burnie to produce Oxford Class Amber Ale, something they have been very successful in doing. Burk is from Maryland, but Stuart-Paul is from England. After careful research, here and in the United Kingdom, they brought over another Englishman, Stephen Parkes, who has a degree in Brewing Sciences, as their brewmaster. Among other things they learned is that there have been more than 200 breweries in the Baltimore area since the 1800s. They use no preservatives, and they do not pasteurize the brew.

You are invited to tour the brewery, either on occasional open house days (usually a Saturday), or with a group. They have a mailing list to notify people of the open house dates and will be glad to enter your name on the list. During the forty-five–minute tour you will see the grain, shipped in from England (with an explanation of the difference between English and American hops), the John Hickey brewing system, brought over from England, the fermenters, two huge cold boxes to store the beer, and the brewing process from mashing to filling the beer kegs. The brewery floor is wet, so wear waterproof shoes with a good tread. The tour usually ends with a little in-house sampling. The British Brewing Company is off New Ordnance Road in Glen Burnie. Call (301) 760–1195 for directions.

For additional information about Anne Arundel County, write to Herman Scheike, Tourism Council of Annapolis and Anne Arundel County, 6 Dock Street, Annapolis 21401, or call (301) 280–0445.

Baltimore City

New Baltimore attractions that deserve your attention are the Great Blacks in Wax Museum (the only one in the country), 1601 East North Avenue, (301) 563–3404; the National Museum of Ceramic Art in Baltimore (the only museum dedicated exclusively to "the celebration of ceramic art"), 250 West Pratt Street, (301) 764–1042; the Indian Cultural Centre, (where you can taste authentic food from India), 110 West Mulberry Street, (301) 528–0333; Baltimore's Holocaust Memorial located at the corner of Gay and Lombard streets; the Jewish Heritage Center on Lloyd Street between Lombard and Baltimore streets, (301) 732–6400; and the Baltimore City Conservatory, Druid Lake Drive, (301) 396–1080.

Our coverage of the city will include two special city views, a new memorial, the traditional painted screens of East Baltimore, two restaurants, and a number of factory tours.

A spectacular way to start your Baltimore visit is at the **Top of the World Trade Center.** On a clear day, you will see an eye-opening, five-sided panoramic view of the city, its harbor, and beyond from the twenty-seventh floor of the tallest pentagonal building in the country, designed by I. M. Pei. Exhibits, films, and audio-visual material will familiarize you with Baltimore's past, present, and future. The World Trade Center is at 401 East Pratt Street. Hours are Monday through Saturday, 10:00 A.M. to 5:00 P.M. and Sunday 12:00 noon to 5:00 P.M.; call about extended summer hours. Admission for adults is $2; for children five to fifteen and seniors, $1. The phone number is (301) 837–4515.

If you would like an organized or specially designed personal tour, then you should call Ruth Fader at Baltimore Rent-A-Tour. Ruth started her business in the early 1970s when she realized no one was giving tours of Baltimore. Now, her company conducts about 900 tours a year. Baltimore Rent-A-Tour specializes in the distinctive. Our favorite is her insomniac tour, which may take you late at night to a bakery, nocturnal zoo animals, a television station preparing for the late-news broadcast, and a newspaper preparing the first edition of tomorrow's breakfast companion.

Another is her Halloween tour (costume dressing optional, with best costume prizes, of course), which may include

Central Maryland

Edgar Allan Poe's grave and the catacombs at the Westminster Church, the ghost of the Shot Tower, and the Baltimore Streetcar Museum, to ride the turn-of-the-century trolleys. This tour ends with a fine view of the sunrise from the "Top of the World" at the Trade Center. Surely, you have the idea by now. Contact Baltimore Rent-A-Tour at 3414 Philips Drive, Baltimore 21208, or call (301) 653–2998.

On May 28, 1989, the **Maryland Viet Nam Veterans Memorial** was dedicated to the 1,046 Marylanders who were killed or missing in action in the Viet Nam conflict. The names and inscriptions are readable whether one is standing, in a wheelchair, or at a child's eye level. The veterans' names are etched into granite, along with this inscription:

> Marylanders, while in this place, pause to recall our nation's ideals, its promise, its abundance, and our continuing responsibilities toward the shared fulfillment of our aspirations. Remember, too, those whose exertions and sacrifices underlie these blessings. Remember, indeed, the living and the dead.

Funds were raised by Maryland veterans who called themselves "The Last Patrol." They marched across the state during a sweltering August heat in 1986, from Oakland in western Maryland to Ocean City in the east, and another 200 miles from Point Lookout to Baltimore the next year. Architect Paul Spreiregan designed the monument. It stands beside the Patapsco River in Middle Branch Park, off Route 2.

Old Baltimore has long been known for its blocks and blocks of row houses, with their brightly scrubbed white marble steps. Almost as historic, but not nearly as well known, are the **painted screens** for windows and doors that decorate the houses lining the streets of East Baltimore.

It is said that William Oktavec painted the first screen on a hot summer day in 1913. His fresh produce was wilting in the heat, so he took it inside and painted groceries on the screens to show his customers what he had available. When you understand that this area is all cement and brick, with very little greenery, no front yards, and few gardens or trees, you can appreciate the thoughts some had about providing a little colorful decoration. Another advantage of the painted

Maryland Viet Nam Veterans Memorial

screens is that windows and doors can be left open for the breezes because the paint allows those who are inside to look out, but outsiders cannot see in.

People started painting on the screens red-roofed bungalows and ponds with ducks or swans swimming around in them. There are rainbows and religious scenes, but mostly the artwork reflects the memories of the inhabitants' home countries in Europe and scenes of a new life in America. The scenes depicted the single-family, country-cottage homes of the sort everyone dreamed of owning.

For the best screen viewing, start at Haussner's Restaurant (see below) and travel along both sides of Eastern Avenue. The Hatton Senior Center, at the corner of Fait and South Linwood avenues, has screens in each of its twenty windows. Remember, this generally is a seasonal display, with the screens in place between May and October.

Six or seven screen painters remain, but they are in their fifties or older. They still work away at it, saying "Practice makes perfect and perfect practice makes art."

You can have a screen painted for about $20 and up, even if you do not live in or visit Baltimore. Write the Painted Screen Society of Baltimore, Box 12122, Baltimore 21281.

Although there are many restaurants of note in Baltimore neighborhoods, including Fell's Point, Little Italy, Charles Street's Restaurant Row, and, of course, Harborplace, at 1727 East Pratt Street, we will highlight two of our favorites.

Both are classics. Taking them alphabetically (the only fair way), we will start with Stuart Attman's favorite place, Attman's Delicatessen. This deli, established in 1915, is the place to go for corned beef sandwiches, knishes, beef barley and mushroom soup ("Bubbie's best"), Dr. Brown's celery tonic, and Attman's "World-Famous Jumbo Kosher Hot Dogs served the way you like it . . . on a real Jewish seeded roll." This is not a kosher delicatessen, for you can also find crab soup and Reuben sandwiches among the menu selections, and the shop is open on Saturday; but it has the feel of one. The store is narrow, crowded, busy, and smells seductively delicious. The choices are puzzling; what do you order first, and should you eat in or carry out? In any case, Attman's has been touted by *Baltimore* magazine as "Baltimore's Best Deli" every year since 1985. We are not about to argue with such experts.

Attman's Delicatessen, 1019 East Lombard Street, Baltimore 21202, is open 8:00 A.M. to 7:00 P.M. daily; call (301) 563–2666. No credit cards. Attman's also can be found at Owings Mills Town Center, 2106 Mill Run Circle, Owings Mills 21117 (301–363–1661), and Pomona Square, Pikesville 21208 (301–484–8477).

Our second choice is Haussner's, where the menu has over one hundred entrees, many of them German specialties. Inspirational desserts are available here or to take home, if you could begin to eat dessert after one of their meals. But Haussner's is equally famous for its extensive original art and antique display.

People have been coming here to this family-owned and operated restaurant to dine and view the paintings, etchings, china, and sculpture by some of Europe's renowned masters since 1926. Here, you can enjoy Baltimore's largest privately-owned art collection and feast on German-American and seafood delicacies. Imagine dining with Rembrandt, Gainsborough, and Whistler! At Haussner's, you can.

Haussner's is located at 3242 Eastern Avenue, Baltimore 21224; call (301) 327–8365. Reservations are accepted for lunch only. Hours are Tuesday through Saturday from 11:00 A.M. to 11:00 P.M.

Now, on to a few fascinating factory tours.

The **General Motors Baltimore Assembly Plant** turns out GMC Safaris and Chevrolet Astros at the rate of nearly one a minute, twenty hours a day, five days a week. In a cavernous room split by railroad tracks and box cars, you can watch a flat piece of stamped sheet metal, instrument panel shells, heater controls, windshields, roofs, carpet (watching water nozzles cut carpet is really interesting), engines, and all the other components come together to form a car.

It is a throbbing, pulsating, noisy, smelly operation, but big and little engineers love to watch it. The tour follows a one-and-a-half-mile-long assembly line and takes about ninety minutes; tours are offered weekdays at 9:00 A.M. and 7:30 P.M. They accept a maximum of fifty people and advise that no cameras are allowed and no open-toe shoes or sandals should be worn. Children must be ten or older, and safety glasses are provided. Reservations with three weeks' notice are requested and can be made by calling Bill McGonigle at

41

(301) 631–2508 or by writing General Motors Baltimore Assembly Plant, P.O. Box 148, 2122 Broening Highway, Baltimore 21203. The plant is located near Sparrows Point. Take Interstate 95 north to Fort McHenry Tunnel, turn right at Boston Street (the first exit after the tunnel), and right again on Broening Highway.

The Eagle Coffee Company, one of the few independent coffee-roasting companies in the United States, sells about one million pounds of coffee a year. You can watch (and smell) the coffee roasting and packaging processes. The free, hour-long tours are offered weekdays by appointment, with twenty-five people maximum. Call Jacqueline Parris at the Eagle Coffee Company, 1019-27 Hillen Street, Baltimore, (301) 685–5893.

The **Calvert Distilling Company** lets you follow the preparation of fine whiskeys, vodka, and gin from distilling through the bottling process to quality control, including a view of the warehouses filled with the finished product and a sampling from a lab technician. Call (301) 247–1000 to reserve a free ninety-minute tour. A maximum of fifty people are permitted on the tour, which is given weekdays by appointment only at the House of Seagrams, 5001 Washington Boulevard, Baltimore 21227.

Our last tour is through the offices of the Pulitzer prize-winning daily newspaper *The Baltimore Sun*. Follow the frantic process from newsroom to composing room to press room. One-hour tours are offered Monday, Wednesday, and Thursday at 9:30 A.M., 11:00 A.M., and 1:00 P.M. by appointment. There is no charge, but your request must be in writing, and they accept no more than thirty people. They do not allow children below the fourth-grade level, and Stuart Boytilla is the person to contact. If you want to talk with him, the best time to call is between 3:00 and 4:00 P.M. *The Baltimore Sun* offices are at 501 North Calvert Street, Baltimore 21278 (301–332–6222).

Kirk Stieff and Moore's Candies no longer offer tours because of insurance restrictions. You may see brochures advertising the tours but you will have to disregard them.

One more note, and that is about the Baltimore Orioles and Memorial Stadium. The "Good Old Stadium" is being replaced by a modern stadium (where archaeologists have unearthed many artifacts) that will look like—a good old stadium. It will not be in a residential area, but it will be closer to the harbor and the interstate highways, and it has already been announced that the 1993 All-Star game will be played here. However, if you plan to visit the old Memorial Stadium and you want an autograph, the best place to wait after the game is in front of the Orioles office or at Gate W2. If you want an autograph from the other team (boo, hiss), wait outside Gate E2.

Baltimore has a subway system and a two-route trolley system, which runs along the Charles Street corridor and around the Inner Harbor area on a daily basis. The trolley costs $.25 (or $20.00 for 100 tickets). The subway, although modern, is not very beneficial for tourists because the stations are not located very close to tourist spots, so stay with the overhead walkways or the trolley system.

For additional Baltimore information, write to Jane White, Media and Public Information Officer, Baltimore Area Convention and Visitors Association, One East Pratt Street, Plaza Level, Baltimore 21202, (301) 659–7300; or contact Barbara Bozzuto, Executive Director, Baltimore Office of Promotion, 34 Market Place, Suite 310, Baltimore 21202, (301) 752–8632. Call (301) 783–1800, extension 6001 for event information, and extension 6002 for attraction information.

Baltimore County

Two post office mural selections are of interest here. The first is in Catonsville, where in 1942 Avery Johnson painted five scenes of historic note, entitled "Incidents of History of Catonsville." The murals start with Indians, go on to farmers rolling tobacco in hogsheads to market, and then depict the romance of Richard Caton and Mary "Holly" Carroll. Holly, the daughter of Declaration of Independence signer Charles Carroll, was only sixteen when Caton proposed. Her father refused because he said Caton had a reputation for not paying his debts. Caton prevailed, and they were married in 1788. Charles Carroll built a house for them, Castle Thunder, on Frederick Road, where the library is now; then he built a newer home in Green Spring Valley (that home still stands). The last panel shows Caton, Holly, and Charles Carroll with his plans for the town of Catonsville.

Several years ago the post office roof began to leak and that did not bode well for the plaster walls or the paintings. The late Thomas Cockey, whose family also goes back to the eighteenth century, decided the murals should be repaired. Federal officials balked at the $35,000 repair bill, but Cockey (as in the town of Cockeysville, also in Baltimore County) and the Historical Society prevailed. A plaque documenting the story depicted in the panels has been installed by the Society.

The Towson Post Office murals caused a real ruckus. Nicolai Cikovsky, a Russian-born, naturalized citizen, was an artist who lived in Washington, D.C. In 1939 he gave the postmaster, at the postal official's request, a series of panels depicting "Milestones in American Transportation." The populace took one look and cried foul. They declared the subject of the paintings was trite, derivative, and cliche. They also were upset by inaccuracies, such as a wagon pulled by horses without reins, smokestack smoke going the wrong direction, a train looking like a model railroad engine rather than a real locomotive, and a gun holster on backwards.

This was the work of a painter who had studied at several distinguished schools in Russia, taught in the U.S. at the Corcoran Gallery, and sold paintings to the Chicago Art Institute, the Whitney Museum of American Art, and numerous other celebrated galleries across the country.

At best, the residents thought the paintings looked like bad "B" movie posters. They wanted murals that reflected the life and history of Towson, and they wanted the artist to visit the area; often artists went to see the location where their painting would hang. Of course, even if the murals did depict the locality, they were not necessarily accurate; one in Barre, Vermont, shows men working in the quarries on stone that has never been found in Vermont and with tools that, even if they were not outdated, were never used in Vermont. The Prince George's County mural in Upper Marlboro, Maryland, is another example.

The upshot is that the errors were corrected, and the murals stayed, where they are to this day. They can be found at 101 West Chesapeake Avenue, Towson. This is no longer the main post office but is now the finance office.

Wild Acres Trail, a new, mile-long wildlife habitat demonstration trail in Owings Mills, was opened in late 1989 in the seventy-two acre Gwynnbrook Wildlife Management Area. It features twenty-three ways to help gardeners and wildlife watchers invite birds, butterflies, and other animals to their property. Trail maps are available for the self-guided tour, and the trail is open from dawn to dusk daily except on Wednesday. No pets are allowed.

Included along the trail are a backyard pond and rock garden; a bee, butterfly, and hummingbird garden; nesting structures for birds and squirrels; bird feeders; and a variety of garden plants that produce fruit eaten by all sorts of animals. Other examples are shown for large property owners.

Over 120 kinds of birds live in or visit the Gwynnbrook area, making bird-watching a marvelous recreational attraction. Photo opportunities are wondrous because of the wildflowers that bloom in the spring and fall.

Maryland Center for Public Broadcasting, the highly regarded public television system of Maryland, offers free tours through their facility, which is at 11767 Bonita Avenue, Owings Mills 21117. Guests who take the thirty- to forty-five–minute tour see the production studios, control room, scene dock area, engineering, and master control. Reservations are by appointment only, and you must sign up at least two weeks in advance. The minimum age is twelve. They will accept groups of ten to forty people. Tours are offered seven days a week at 10:00 A.M., 2:00 P.M., and 7:00 P.M., except during November, December, March, and August because of fund raising and membership drives. Call Kathleen Rumbley, Volunteer Coordinator, (301) 581–4264 or (800) 223–3678 from nearby states.

At the Towson State University, in the Fine Arts Center, is the **Asian Arts Center** at the Roberts Gallery, named in honor of Frank Roberts, who donated a large number of Asian artifacts and artworks to start this collection. Changing and permanent displays of Asian, African, and pre-Columbian works are featured. Concerts, films, lectures, and workshops are sponsored throughout the school year.

The Asian Arts Center is open June through August, Monday through Friday 11:00 A.M. to 3:00 P.M.; September through May, Monday through Friday 10:00 A.M. to 4:00 P.M.,

45

and Sunday 2:00 to 4:30 P.M. No admission is charged. Groups come by appointment. Call (301) 830–2807.

The **Oregon Ridge Park and Nature Center** is a great place to take a break after hours of driving and seeing regular tourist attractions. Within its 836 acres are a number of marked trails of varying length and difficulty, downhill and cross-country skiing areas, a greenhouse, an archaeological research site, an outdoor stage, and a launching site for hang gliders.

Starting in the nature center, you can see how a honeybee hive works, look at local flowers and plants in the greenhouse, or check on live animals, such as fish, frogs, mice, salamanders, snakes, and Stubby, the pet opposum, all native to the park. A huge tree exhibit reveals the various parts of the forest ecosystem, from worms and moles living among the roots and underbrush to the owls and hawks perching in its highest limbs. The area's history is depicted by artifacts retrieved from archaeological digs in the park. These items were reclaimed from the digs by students in the Baltimore County public school system. They also work to construct a full-scale replica of an 1850s storage shed, set on its original foundation outside the nature center.

The nature trails criss-cross the park, so a hiker sees the natural process of birds, fields, ponds, streams, swamps, wildlife, and woods. For those who like nature on the cultured side, summer concerts are presented by the Baltimore Symphony.

Oregon Ridge Park and Nature Center, Beaver Dam Road, is reached by the Shawan Road Exit 20-B off Interstate 83; go west 1 mile, turn left on Beaver Dam Road, bear right at the fork and follow the signs. Call (301) 771–0034 for more information.

Ashland Furnace is one of the six relatively easily reached furnaces in Maryland (the others are Catoctin Furnace, Lanaconing Iron Furnace, Antietam, Principio in Cecil County, and Nassawango in Worcester County). Said to have been named for the Kentucky home of Henry Clay, its three furnaces, engine room, and a casting house were kept functioning from around 1844 to 1893. Additionally there were large storage buildings for raw materials and a village with a school, church, store, and about five dozen houses.

The ore was mined from Phoenix, Glencoe, Riderwood, Texas, Oregon Ridge, and other parts of what is now north-central Baltimore County. Now the area has been mined by a developer, and the Strutt Group has incorporated about a dozen of the old village's buildings. The office and mid-nineteenth century store, the school, several houses, and a group of dwellings called Stone Row have been renovated and assimilated into their industrial site. The old Ashland Presbyterian Church, near the gates of the new community, is still an active place of worship.

Ashland Furnace is east on Paper Mill Road from York Road, just north of Cockeysville.

For additional tourism information write to Susan Seifried, Director, Office of Promotion and Tourism, or Laurie Fitzgibbons, Assistant, Courthouse Mezzanine, Towson 21204 or call (301) 887–8040.

Carroll County

This county was named for Charles Carroll, an American Revolutionary leader and Maryland signer of the Declaration of Independence.

If you are coming to Carroll County, most likely you are driving along Interstate 70 to or from Baltimore, or you are here to visit the Carroll County Farm Museum and to stop by the International Gift Shop, 500 Main Street, New Windsor (301–635–2111). If you sign the guest book at the tourist information center (210 East Main Street, Westminster 301–848–1388), you will receive a gift from the gift shop.

As long as you are here, though, you should check with the **Hashawha Environmental Appreciation Center** in Westminster. Hashawha is an Indian term meaning "old fields," which certainly describes this area.

Hashawha, a tranquil 420-acre park, is part of the Carroll County Department of Recreation and Parks and serves as a resource for environmental education and outdoor recreation. During the school year, all sixth-graders spend a week at Hashawha in an "outdoor classroom."

Recreational opportunities include fishing, bird-watching, biking, and cross-country skiing. A wilderness camping area, for which reservations are needed, is located along the 4.5-mile trail system. Other attractions include a partially restored 1850 log cabin and play areas.

Special events are scheduled throughout the year, such as the Maple Sugaring Festival in March, the Honeybee Festival in September, and the Nature Art Show and Sale in December. Summer concerts in the park, lectures, and festivals are free of charge; other programs have a modest charge.

The Maple Sugaring Festival is particularly interesting for two reasons. First, it is something to do to get you out of the house in early March after hibernating all winter. Second, it lets you know about the maple sugaring industry—for example, that Maryland is the tenth-leading maple manufacturing state in the country. The festival features taste testing, films, related country crafts, a food concession, and fun for the whole family. A special attraction is wagon rides to the pioneer log cabin courtesy of the Maryland Horse and Mule Team Association. Admission is free.

The meeting rooms, cafeteria, nature discovery area, five winterized cabins (accommodating twenty-eight people each), in-ground swimming pool, and a solar-heated conference center seating 150 people are available for public use on a reservation basis. Hashawha is at 300 John Owings Road, off Route 97, north of Westminster. Call (301) 848–9040 or 848–9566.

Carroll County's streams, valleys, farms, woodlands, and villages provide an ideal backdrop for exploring off the highway, and an ideal way to do that is by bicycle. **Bicycle tours** have been designed by resident cyclists outlining ten of their favorite routes, ranging from short to long and easy to challenging. Each route is on a separate map with its own description of the tour. Brochures are available for $1 at the tourist information center in Westminster.

For example, the Taneytown route is nearly 14 miles long with a moderately hilly ride. It starts at Taneytown Memorial Park, "where a public pool and picnic grounds offer warm weather possibilities. Your tour heads toward Littlestown, Pennsylvania, and winds through rustic areas where deer and pheasants abound. Pick out an early Christmas tree at one of the tree farms, or stop and listen to the ripplings of

Pipe Creek. Wind back through the alleys of Taneytown and by the beautiful Fish and Game club pond."

The New Windsor tour has rolling hills and is 8 miles long "Wind through the beautiful Wakefield Valley on your way past Robert Strawbridge's Home (birthplace of American Methodism). This ride offers splendid country scenery, picturesque seventeenth- and eighteenth-century homes and an opportunity to stop at the New Windsor Service Center and visit its unique International Gift Shop."

According to local legend, you and we are not the only visitors to Carroll County. Several apparitions also frequent the countryside, and you may even meet a friendly one. The first of the **Ghosts of Carroll County** is at the Shellman House, 210 East Main Street, Westminster. A little girl in white, they say, delights at having visitors stop by the tourist center, located at the Historical Society of Carroll County. Spirits, in addition to the liquid kind, are said to reside at Cockey's Tavern, 216 East Main Street; starting in the early 1800s, this tavern has been the site of political rallies for Andrew Jackson, anti-tax meetings, fancy balls, and all-night debauchery.

At Main and Court streets, the ghosts of slaves supposedly return to the Carroll County auction block where slave trading was done in pre-revolutionary war times. Other specters have been reported at Ascension churchyard, the Courthouse, the old Westminster jail, Western Maryland College (Levine Hall has a musical ghost), and Avondale—the home of Legh Master, the most celebrated of Carroll's ghosts—on Stone Chapel Road in Wakefield Valley. It is said that Master was a tyrant, a miser, a lecher, and a cad. Two Confederate ghosts reportedly visit the last remaining building of Irving College on Grafton Street, and on the full moon, an Indian walks a ridge in the tiny town of Lineboro.

For those of you who choose to pursue these nocturnal visitors, talk with the Historical Society in general (through the Office of Promotion and Tourism) and Amos Davidson, a local historian, in particular. Additional tourism information is available from the Carroll County Office of Promotion and Tourism; write to Micki Smith, Director, County Office Building, 225 North Center Street, Westminster 21157, or call (301) 876–2085, extension 2973.

Cecil County

If you have watched movies such as *The Manchurian Candidate*, *Guys & Dolls*, *The Philadelphia Story*, *Pillow Talk*, and *Solid Gold Cadillac*, then you have heard people talking about eloping to Elkton or going to "that town in Maryland" to get married. Up until the late thirties, the town of Elkton was known as the marriage capital of the world. Some 10,000 people a year were wed here, and one assumes most of them were eloping. They came to Elkton because it was the first county seat south of New York and other northeastern areas that did not require a waiting period or blood test before the ceremony was performed.

Only one wedding chapel remains, the Little Wedding Chapel. This is where Babe Ruth and Joan Fontaine were married, among dozens of notables, and this is where nearly 1,000 couples are married each year. Stop by to talk with Barbara Foster and hear some of her many stories, witness a wedding or two, or plan for your own nuptials to be held here.

The **Little Wedding Chapel** is located at 142 East Main Street, Elkton 21921. The phone number is (301) 398–3640.

As long as we are on a romantic subject, we can visit two **covered bridges** (or "kissing" bridges) in Cecil. There was a time when Cecil and Frederick counties vied for the most covered bridges in the state, but few remain.

Gilpin's Falls covered bridge has a 119-foot span and a 13.5-foot roadway, and it is adjacent to Route 272 over Northeast Creek, a half-mile north of Bayview. Reportedly, the bridge's arches were made from single timbers, which were warped to shape by balancing them on stumps and pulling their ends down. It was constructed in the 1850s, abandoned in the 1930s, and left to disintegrate until 1959, when it was restored. Traffic along Route 272 bypasses the bridge, which is within a few yards of the roadway.

Gilpin's Falls covered bridge, 5 miles north of the town of North East, or 2 miles north of Interstate 95, on Route 272.

The second covered bridge is at Fair Hill, which was a 7,000-acre estate owned by William DuPont, Jr.; the entire Maryland portion, more than 5,000 acres, was purchased by the state as a Natural Resource Area. In the northern reaches of the property, near the Pennsylvania border, is the 1850s covered bridge, which has been on private property for years. Until recently, to find it, you had to wander through the Fair Hill Condominiums (for thoroughbred racehorses) along roads posted against trespassers and hope you could find your way through the twists and turns and lack of directional signs.

Dan Brower, who manages this natural resource area, was pleased to tell us that the bridge soon will be accessible to the public, and the old stone manor house will be open as a nature center (run in cooperation with the Cecil County Government and the Fair Hill Environmental Association); the dedication ceremonies were set for April 22, 1990, in honor of the twentieth anniversary of the first Earth Day. Eventually, a new, more direct road will be opened to the bridge, which is in very good condition. Brower says there are two Mason-Dixon markers on the property, and he hopes one of the earliest activities will be to clear the way to the stones so that they will be more accessible.

The Fair Hill Condominiums were mentioned, and any activity you see around here probably has to do with some very monied horse fanciers and prize-winning horses. Fox hunts are held on these grounds about four or five days a week between fall and spring. You can hike or follow the riding trails, but check into the office first to make sure you will not be crossing paths with others.

Across Route 273 is the steeplechase track at Fair Hill, an exact replica of Aintree, where England's Grand National is held. Since it opened in 1933, there have been a number of steeplechase races annually, and the May and September events are the only steeplechase races in the United States that permit parimutuel wagering. Fair Hill is also the home of the National Steeplechase and Hunt Association, which moved from Belmont, New York, in June 1989.

Fair Hill Natural Resource Management Area is at the junction of Route 273 and Route 213, Fair Hill 21921. Call (301) 398–1246.

The Mitchell House is a two-and-a-half–story stone dwelling believed to have been built in 1764 (based on a fireback date), though it has had considerable alterations since that date; it is the location of the **Fair Hill Inn.** The house

51

has been a Revolutionary War hospital for Continental soldiers (run by its owner, Dr. Abraham Mitchell), a hotel, a post
office, and a store. Mr. and Mrs. Anthony Graziano purchased it from the state of Maryland in 1978 when it was in a
dilapidated condition and proudly restored it.

Now the house is a fine restaurant that features an Italian
continental menu but specializes in Maryland seafood. Just
perusing the menu, which includes Veal Imperial (a Fair Hill
delight), Pasta Marinara (scallops, shrimp, clams, and mussels, served over pasta), and Seafood Beatrice (lobster tail,
scallops, shrimp, and crabmeat cooked with brandy, flamed
with Pernod, for two), is enough to encourage *buon appetito.*

The Fair Hill Inn is open for lunch, Tuesday through Friday
from 11:30 A.M. to 2:30 P.M., for dinner, Tuesday through Sunday from 5:00 to 9:00 P.M., and for Sunday brunch, from
11:30 A.M. to 2:30 P.M. Reservations are advised; call (301)
398–4187. The inn is located at routes 273 and 213, Fair Hill
21921.

At one time there were two covered bridges crossing the
Susquehanna River, but the last one was flooded with the
construction of the **Conowingo Hydroelectric Plant.** Built
in 1928, Conowingo is one of the largest hydroelectric plants
in the northeast, if not in the country. The enormous dam
forms a freshwater lake 14 miles long, impounding some 105
billion gallons of water. It is a noted freshwater fishing spot.

The best part is that you can see the plant tick. On weekends you don't need an appointment; just show up at the
entrance below the station on the downriver side at 9:30
A.M., 11:00 A.M., 1:00 P.M., or 2:30 P.M. Somebody will be there
to show you through the dam, where you will see the genera-
tors, pumps, air tanks, water pipelines, transformers, circuit
breakers, high-tension wires, and all kinds of electrical
equipment. Children must be twelve or older to take the
entire tour, but younger children will be allowed in to see
part of the operation. You should not wear high heels
because there are a lot of grates to walk over.

Daily and group tour reservations should be made a week
or more in advance, and groups should be no larger than
forty people. The tour must be taken between 8:00 A.M. and
4:00 P.M., so you should schedule the one-hour-plus tour no
later than 2:30 P.M. Call the recreation office at (301)

457–2400. The address is Conowingo Dam, Route 1, Conowingo 21918.

Established in 1876, the **Day Basket Factory** in the town of North East still makes oak splint baskets the old-fashioned way. Shortly after the Civil War, Edward and Samuel Day came to North East from Massachusetts to make their baskets because the wood was plentiful, the transportation was good, and the demand for their wares, particularly from cotton pickers, was great.

Business boomed, and during World War I the factory had thirty-five people on its payroll turning out 2,000 baskets a week. In November of 1989 Robert and Virginia McKnight, Dean Richwine, Theodore Lambert III, and Gary Sorrelle bought the factory. There are four or five basket makers there who produce old-time baskets, from lunch and market styles, to fruit and bread baskets. Hobbyists will be pleased to know they have pliable number 1 oak strips, hand split in any dimension, for chair seats, or baskets, or whatever need.

You can watch the process (you must be at least eighteen) Monday through Friday between 8:30 A.M. and 4:00 P.M. The store is open on Saturday, but on that day there are no workers there. Please call ahead (301–287–6100) to let them know if you will want a tour. The factory, located at 110 West High Street, North East 21901, is closed in January and February.

Plumpton Park Zoo is a small, rural zoological garden that features plants as well as exotic and native animals, including emu, wallabies, llamas, bison, Persian sheep, Chinese deer, miniature donkeys, Pygmy goats, wild turkies, and Australian Black Swans, in a country setting. Eighteenth-century buildings and ruins are on the grounds, including the 1734 mill that houses the gift shop. The zoo has an adopt-an-animal program, with prices ranging from $10 for an African goose to $100 for a zebra.

Plumpton Park Zoo is open from 10:00 A.M. to 5:00 P.M. daily. Adults are $2 and children are $1. Group tours are available. Contact the zoo at 1416 Telegraph Road (Route 273), Rising Sun 21911, or call (301) 658–6350.

With over 200 miles of tidal shoreline, dozens of marinas, and acres of waterfront parks, all poised at the top of the Chesapeake Bay, it is easy to understand the importance of the estuary in the history of this county. The creation of the

Chesapeake and Delaware Canal on October 17, 1829 made water transportation in this area even more important. At that time the canal had four locks, but the Army Corps of Engineers lowered the canal to sea level in 1927.

Receiving considerably less publicity than the C & O Canal, the 13-mile C & D Canal cuts off some 350 miles of water navigation for ships going between Philadelphia and Baltimore, and the 22,000 vessels that use it annually make it one of the busiest waterways in the world.

A museum in Chesapeake City, located next to the canal, reviews its history; it is open Monday through Saturday from 8:00 A.M. to 4:15 P.M. and Sunday from 10:00 A.M. to 6:00 P.M. The museum is closed on Sunday from Thanksgiving through Easter. Call (301) 885–5622 for more information.

We find the other, or north, side of the canal much more interesting. During the ride or walk across the bridge, 135 feet in the air, you can see the canal's course for miles in both directions. From the north side of the canal you can see the pilots on their pilot boats going to and from the ships navigating the canal. Stop by the Pilot House for information and a schedule on ships coming through.

To help pass the time, either waiting to watch the current change with the tide, or waiting for a ship to come through, stop in at **Schaefer's Canal House**, a popular Chesapeake Bay landmark since 1917, for fine canal-side dining on crab delicacies. You also will find weekday specials, such as Monday's all-you-can-eat prime rib, Tuesday's shrimp, Wednesday's land-and-sea platter for two, and Thursday's seafood buffet. If you are at all undecided, try the Cioppino, not exactly a Chesapeake specialty, but a San Francisco one that offers shrimp, clams, scallops, lobster, and crabmeat served with French bread.

Owner Gunter C. Sunkler says he prides himself in "using only the best products and the finest ingredients available. We serve only fresh meats, seafood and vegetables, as well as fresh whipped cream. All our soups, sauces, and pastries are made on the premises." Desserts are made fresh daily by chef Larry Sunkler, who trained in Salzburg, Austria for four years.

Nautical decorations prevail, with many old photographs of the area and a model of the thirty-four-ton Home Lines cruise ship *Oceanic* commemorating its passage through the canal on its maiden voyage to the Bahamas in April 1965. A gift shop is open from April 1 through December 1.

The restaurant is at 208 Bank Street, Chesapeake City 21915. It is open Monday through Saturday 11:00 A.M. to 10:00 P.M. and Sunday 11:00 A.M. to 9:00 P.M. A Sunday brunch is served from 11:00 A.M. to 3:00 P.M. Call (301) 885–2200. Docking is available.

For additional tourism information, write to Mrs. Ruth Cameron, Tourism Director, Economic Development Office, Room 300, County Office Building, Elkton 21921, or call (301) 398–0200, extension 144.

Harford County

Harford County goes from covered bridge to lighthouse, which explains the variety of features you will find here.

One of the remaining covered bridges in Maryland connects Harford and Baltimore counties and crosses over Gunpowder Falls. The **Jerusalem Covered Bridge** was constructed between 1850 and 1860 and measures 88 feet, with a 14.7-foot roadway. Steel beams, steel stringers, steel cross tie rods, and bottom chord were installed at a later date for reinforcement, and today it remains in good condition. To reach the bridge, take Route 24 and turn left onto Jerusalem Road to Jericho Road.

Havre de Grace (pronounced as it is spelled, not with a French pronunciation) is the home of the oldest continuously used lighthouse on the east coast. The Concord Point Light was constructed in 1827 but decommissioned in 1975; it was later vandalized but is now in tip-top shape. You can climb the twenty-eight steps plus six steps on a ladder and have an impressive view of the Susquehanna River and the Chesapeake Bay.

The lighthouse is open on Saturday and Sunday afternoons from 1:00 to 5:00 P.M., May through October, or by appointment. It is located on Lafayette Street in Havre de Grace. The phone number is (301) 939–1340 or 939–2016.

Another interesting attraction is the Susquehanna Museum of Havre de Grace, which tells you about the Southern Terminal of the Susquehanna and Tidewater Canal. The museum's

Concord Point Light

address is P.O. Box 253, Havre de Grace 21078 (301–939–5780).

A self-guided tour brochure is available from Harford County Tourism in Belair; it highlights a sample of the 800 structures that contribute to the Havre de Grace Historic District. The buildings range in period from the 1780s through the Canal era (1830–1850) and the Victorian era (1880–1910) to the contemporary.

Havre de Grace is the self-proclaimed decoy capital of the world, and the Havre de Grace Decoy Museum has complete collections of decoys by Madison Mitchell and Paul Gibson. An annual Decoy Festival is held about the first weekend of May at the museum and the Havre de Grace Middle School. The Decoy Museum is open Tuesday through Sunday from 11:00 A.M. to 4:00 P.M. and by appointment; the address is R. Madison Mitchell Place, Havre de Grace 21078. Call (301) 939–1800 or 939–5780.

About ten blocks up the road, at Franklin Street and North Union Avenue, is the **Susquehanna Trading Company.** Owner Duane Henry has more than 2,500 old and new Chesapeake Bay decoys on display and locally handcrafted decoys for sale, starting at $9.95. He also features a large selection of waterfowl decorations, including miniature decoys; wildlife-decorated personal, household, and office accessories; limited-edition prints; and decoy lamps. The Susquehanna Trading Company is open seven days a week from 10:00 A.M. to 5:00 P.M. at 322 North Union Avenue, (301) 939–4252.

Crossing the Susquehanna River is the Thomas J. Hatem Memorial Bridge, between Harford and Cecil counties. It opened in 1940 as the Susquehanna River Bridge and was renamed in 1986 to honor Hatem, a prominent Harford County resident who devoted his life to public and civic service. The bridge is 1.5 miles long and 89 feet above the river, connecting the communities of Havre de Grace and Perryville. More than seven million vehicles use the bridge each year. The toll is $1 for passenger cars.

Liriodendron is a Palladian-style mansion with Greek columns, French doors, marble walls in the kitchen and bathroom, and thirteen fireplaces; it is now on the National Register of Historic Places. It was built as a palatial summer home in 1898 for Dr. Howard A. Kelly, one of the "Big Four" founders of Baltimore's Johns Hopkins Hospital and Medical School. This historic house museum features changing exhibits and art displays as well as a permanent exhibit of memorabilia from the Kelly Collection. Now it is a cultural center for Harford County, with superb facilities for exhibitions, lectures, and concerts.

Tours are available on Sunday from 1:00 to 5:00 P.M. except on national holidays. Call (301) 838–3942 or 879–4424. The address is Liriodendron, 502 West Gordon Street, Bel Air 21014.

For additional tourism information write to Clifton Dowling, Tourism Coordinator, Harford County Office of Economic Development, Festival at Bel Air, Suite P-1611, 5 Bel Air Parkway South, Bel Air 21014, or call (301) 879–2000, extension 339 or 838–6000, extension 339.

Howard County

Howard County offers tremendous contrasts in life-styles: from Ellicott City, a former mill town, with its original stone buildings, antique and specialty shops, historic sites, and B & O (Baltimore and Ohio) Railroad Station Museum; to Columbia, the planned village, with its Merriweather Post Pavilion, huge mall, and Columbia Exhibit Center. As usual, we will cover some of the less-visited and more countrified places.

Although not a covered bridge, the Bollman Truss Bridge (1869) is of interest because the red, cast-iron, open railroad bridge is the only one of its type in the world. It is said to be the first bridge constructed of iron, as opposed to wood or stone. Restoration of the bridge took place in 1974, near Savage Mill (which is now filled with antique shops and artist's studios), and there is a nice little park and hiking trails around the bridge. You can find the bridge off Route 1, at Savage, near Savage Mill.

Another bridge of note was and is for trains rather than cars. The **Thomas Viaduct** (1833) stretches from Baltimore County to Howard County across the Patapsco River. Eight elliptical arches support a 60-foot high granite block structure, which allowed tall ships to pass under. Just as the Ellicott City Railroad Station has endured as a landmark to the growth of railroading in Maryland, so does the viaduct.

When B & O Railroad officials began looking to expand the railroad south to Washington, D.C., they faced a monumental problem: how to cross the Patapsco River. They solved it with a monumental structure, the Thomas Viaduct. Named for Philip Thomas, the first president of B & O Railroad, it was designed by Baltimorean Benjamin Latrobe, and it was the first curved, stone-arched bridge in America. Construction began July 4, 1832, and it was completed exactly three years later at a cost of a little over $142,000. It still carries passenger and freight trains.

Picnic areas are in nearby Patapsco State Park. The viaduct is off Levering Avenue in Elkridge.

Away from bridges and on to farms. We cover a few farm market stands and pick-your-own farms in Frederick County, but the **Cider Mill Farm** and **Larriland Farms** are more than that.

Historic Cider Mill Farm (1916) has organic produce, dried flowers, herbs, pies, honey, and other country goods from mid-September through December 24 and January through mid-April. During the apple season they offer guided tours of the cider-making process, including antique hand- and electric-press demonstrations where children can participate, and free cider samples. Tom Owens, the owner, says you can bring your own jug for fresh cider if you like.

Weekend activities include face painting, marble and yo-yo presentations, apple butter making, wine making, a train whistle contest, scarecrow making, beekeeping, storytelling by James Whitcomb Riley, pumpkin carving (bring your own tools and a blanket), and a teddy bear contest (bring your own bear). Remember to bring your camera. A schedule of contests and activities is available.

The Cider Mill Farm is open 10:00 A.M. to sunset, 5012 Landing Road (off Montgomery Road, Route 103) Elkridge 21227; call (301) 788–9595 or 775–0696.

Larriland Farms has a pick-your-own season starting in late May or early June with strawberries and ending with a cut-your-own season for Christmas trees in December. Additionally, the farm has succulent and delicious fruits, vegetables, country hams, and flowers. The market is in a 125-year-old post-and-beam barn. Larriland Farms, owned and operated by G. Laurence Moore, also has hayrides, evening campfires, and other programs that let city folk enjoy the pleasures of a rural life.

The farm is open May through August, Monday through Friday 8:00 A.M. to 8:00 P.M. and September through October, Monday through Friday 9:00 A.M. to 5:00 P.M. Weekend hours are Saturday 9:00 A.M. to 5:00 P.M. and Sunday 10:00 A.M. to 5:00 P.M. Call for December weekend hours. The mailing address is 2955 Florence Road, Woodbine 21797. By car, Larriland Farms (2415 Route 94, Woodbine) is 3 miles south of Interstate 70 (Exit 73) on Route 94, near Lisbon. Their phone number is (301) 489–7034; in season you can call (301) 442–2605 or (301) 854–6110 for a recording of what fruits and vegetables are available.

Toby's the Dinner Theatre of Columbia celebrates the creative genius of Toby Orenstein and her dedication to fine theatrical productions. All the time she is working to entertain you, she is working to teach her "kids" the hows and whys of show business so that they can go on to professional careers in entertainment if they wish.

Dinner at Toby's is an all-you-can-eat buffet that features prime roast beef, steamed shrimp, fresh salad and vegetables, and a dessert table. The most interesting aspect of Toby's is the theater, which has performances in the round. You are never far from the action. The productions may be an outstanding Broadway show from years gone by, such as *Funny Girl*; the latest off the Great White Way, such as *Singin' In the Rain*; or an entirely new attraction, such as a musical version of *It's a Wonderful Life*, which was created at Toby's and offered during the 1989 holiday season. Other selections have included *The Pirates of Penzance, Sunday in the Park with George,* and *Ain't Misbehavin'.*

Toby's is at the South Entrance Road, one-half block west of Route 29, Columbia. The phone numbers are (301) 730–8311; (301) 596–6161 (in Washington); (301) 995–1969 (in Baltimore); and (800) 88TOBYS (in Maryland and surrounding states).

For additional information, write to Barry Bogage, Director, Howard County Economic Development Office, 3430 Court

House Drive, Ellicott City 21043 (301–992–2027); or write to Colleen Riley, Executive Director, Howard County Tourism Council, Columbia Hilton, 5485 Twin Knolls Road, Columbia 21045 (301–730–7817).

Off the Beaten Path in Greater Washington

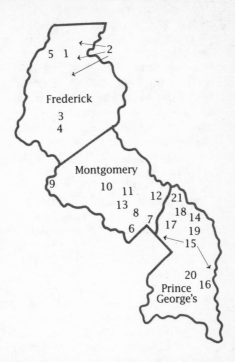

1. Apple and peach orchards
2. Covered bridges
3. *Frederick News Post*
4. Mount Olivet Cemetery
5. Campgrounds
6. Pioneer Lady statue
7. Penguin Rush Hour Mural
8. Post Office Mural
9. White's Ferry
10. Roy's Place
11. Olney Theatre
12. Burn Brae Dinner Theatre
13. Harlequin Dinner Theatre
14. Greenbelt
15. Post Office Murals
16. DuVall Tool Collection
17. Poultry Hall of Fame
18. Patuxent Wildlife Research Center
19. China Pearl
20. Mount Airy Plantation
21. Petrucci's Dinner Theatre

Greater Washington

Frederick, Montgomery, and Prince George's comprise the Greater Washington counties. Washington, D.C., is at the center of a huge suburban megalopolis formed by the blending of these three counties, which work to maintain separate community identities.

Frederick has been a rural farm community, and its pastoral attributes are still there, but the closeness and convenience to Washington are bringing it, perhaps unwillingly, into the next century. Rural enclaves can be found in Montgomery and Prince George's counties; much of this acreage is preserved by Program Open Space projects and the topography, which prohibits construction and human intrusion.

As a native and near-native of this area, we have received a steady stream of visitors over the years who want to tour Washington. We take them to the station and the metro takes them downtown to the many Smithsonian buildings, galleries, the zoo, or anything else they want to see. It is as clean and safe as any subway system around and at last count was the second or third busiest subway in the country.

There are two lines running in Prince George's County, the Blue and the Orange, and one line with two branches running in Montgomery County—the Red Line.

Orange Line stations are located at New Carrollton, Landover, and Cheverly; Blue Line stations are at Addison Road and Capital Heights; and Red Line stations are at Shady Grove, Rockville, Twinbrook, White Flint, Grosvenor, Medical Center, and Bethesda going in toward Washington, and Takoma Park, Silver Spring, Forest Glen, and Wheaton coming out the more northerly route.

Trains run from 5:30 A.M. to midnight on weekdays; from 8:00 A.M. to midnight on Saturday; and 10:00 A.M. to midnight on Sunday. Trains run about every five to fifteen minutes, depending on the time of day. Fares are based on time and distance, with rush hour (5:30 A.M. to 9:30 A.M. and 3:00 P.M. to 7:00 P.M., weekdays) costing more than off-peak times. For a bicycle permit, call (202) 962–1116. For general information about Metro Rail and Metro Bus (such as how to get from your door to your destination), call (202) 637–7000. This number is operational from 6:00 A.M. to 11:30 P.M. daily.

Of course, our book is designed for people who are interested in seeing sights other than the subway. In the Greater Washington area you will find orchards, covered bridges, historic cemeteries, campgrounds, murals, a ferry, places to eat and to be entertained, old farm tools, and a museum dedicated to poultry, among other things.

Frederick County

Frederick County is renowned in certain circles for the antique shops in New Market and Frederick; the restored train depot and museum at Brunswick; the Barbara Fritchie and Roger B. Taney homes; the Byrd Winery and Berrywine plantations; the Catoctin Mountains (where Camp David, the presidential retreat, is located); the Grotto of Lourdes and the St. Elizabeth Ann Seton Shrine; the Lilypons Water Gardens; Governor Thomas Johnson's Rose Hill Manor and Schifferstadt; the many churches and steeples; and, of course, that picturesque stopping point, Sugar Loaf Mountain. Still, there are other treasures here, in this, the largest county in the state.

Driving through, on interstate or back roads and particularly along Route 15, you are sure to notice the hundreds of acres of **apple and peach orchards.** The fruits of their labors are sold to the public, along with preserves, jams, country crafts, and candy. Four of these orchards deserve some notice; all are located adjacent to or just off Route 15.

Catoctin Mountain Orchard is known for its diversity and quality of every type of berry, soft fruit, apples, and vegetables. Cortland, Red and Golden Delicious, Stayman, York, and Ida Red apples are available in autumn. On weekends, however, the supply is not always sufficient for the demand; therefore, they suggest you call early in the day to reserve your fruit. You can pick your own blackberries, black raspberries, sour and sweet cherries, and strawberries between June 1 and August 25, but call ahead for picking days and hours. Catoctin Mountain Orchard also offers preserved fruit and jam, packed in appealing, reusable containers. The orchard is open daily July 1 through January, and Friday, Saturday, and Sunday from January through April. It is closed May 1 through mid-July. You can find the orchard on Route 15, North Franklinville Road, and the mailing address is 15307 Kelbaugh Road, Thurmont 21788. Call (301) 271–2737.

Bell Hill Farm Market and Orchard is a hundred-acre farm, and the family-run fruit stand sits by a pre-Civil War home and stone springhouse. The McKissick family features the traditional Red and Yellow Delicious and Stayman apples, as well as some older varieties, including Grimes Golden, York, Jonathan, and Winesap. In season you can buy peaches, plums, pears, nectarines, watermelons, cantaloupes, raspberries, corn, beans, cucumbers, potatoes, and other produce. Bell Hill Farm is 1½ miles north of Thurmont on Route 15 and is open daily from 9:00 A.M. to 5:00 P.M. Call (301) 271–7264.

Gateway Orchard Roadside Market (Thurmont means "gateway to the mountains") offers locally-grown fruit and some convenience foods. More than 125 varieties of candy are mixed and bagged in their "Candyland." During apple season, you may draw your own cider from their barrels. The market is open seven days a week 9:00 A.M. to 6:00 P.M., year-round. Call (301) 271–2322.

Pryor's Orchard has a modern storage facility housed in a rustic barn-type market, complete with racks of antlers and an antique cider press. Pryor's seventy-three acres is one of the oldest of the Thurmont area orchards, and a favorite of local canning enthusiasts. Pryor's is noted for its many varieties of peaches, summer and fall apples, and pears. You can pick your own sour and sweet cherries and blueberries. The orchard is closed in the winter. It is located ½ mile west of Thurmont on Pryor's Road (take a left off Route 77). Call (301) 271–2693.

You can buy fresh fruit and vegetables or pick your own at some sixty or seventy farms and orchards in fourteen counties across the state, from Anne Arundel to Washington (listed alphabetically, not geographically). Write to George Roche, Marketing Resource and Development Group, Maryland Department of Agriculture, Annapolis 21401, for a copy of the current "Pick your own and Direct Farm Markets in Maryland" brochure. Or stop by a library or county extension office to pick up a copy.

There are three **covered bridges** still in use in Frederick County. The first is Loy's Station, which retains the original 90-foot span and a 12.5-foot roadway; it has a load limit of 6,000 pounds. The original beams and supports of the Howe Truss are still in place; however, the 1850 bridge has been structurally modified. The bridge, which crosses Owens Creek and is surrounded by a five-and-a-half–acre park, is located on Old Frederick Road, off Route 77, 3 miles from Thurmont.

Roddy Road Covered Bridge (1856), near Thurmont, is considered the best looking of the state's remaining bridges by covered bridge fans. It is a single span, about 40 feet long, with a 13.8-foot roadway. It is a fine example of basic king-post truss design, though it has had steel stringers installed at a later date. Surrounding the bridge, which crosses Owens Creek, is a seventy-acre natural area for picnicking and gentle afternoon outings.

The Utica Covered Bridge is the largest of the three. Built in 1850, it was moved in 1889, and has been structurally reinforced with concrete piers and steel beam supports. The bridge used to cross the Monocacy River until a summer flood in 1889 lifted the span from its abutments and placed it down on the river several yards away. Instead of replacing the still-intact bridge on its supports, it was dismantled, moved, and reassembled over Fishing Creek at Utica Mills. The bridge is located on Utica Road off Old Frederick Road, which is off Route 15.

Thurmont originally was called Mechanicstown because Jacob Weller and his family settled here in 1751, and he was a mechanic of German descent. When President Eisenhower suggested our cities develop "sister" cities in foreign countries, local newspaper editor George Wyerman decided his town should have a sister city. Because of its German background, Thurmont selected the town of Stelzenberg, which is geographically similar to Thurmont, and from which many Thurmont settlers emigrated. In July 1988, twenty-five West Germans came to visit and started the citizens of Thurmont talking about an exchange program with Germany.

Thurmont is not only the gateway to the mountains, but the gateway to Camp David. It was originally called High Catoctin and was one of three camps built by the Civilian Conservation Corps during the depression. The other two camps, still in existence, are Misty Mount, used for group camping, and Greentop, used by the Baltimore League of the Handicapped since 1937. The camps were built from local timber.

High Catoctin was renamed Shangri La by Franklin Delano Roosevelt, and then renamed Camp David by Dwight D. Eisenhower. You cannot visit Camp David, but you may be able to drive by Misty Mount or Greentop to see the basic architectural style before presidential changes.

Between Thurmont and Frederick is the old Catoctin Furnace. For 125 years, this was a prosperous iron-making community. Started by a group of men that included the future first governor of Maryland, Thomas Johnson, the stack went into blast in 1776 to produce pig iron, tools, and household items, including the popular ten-plate stove. Bombshells for 10-inch mortars were produced toward the end of the revolutionary war.

By the mid-eighteenth century, the owner of the furnace had eighty houses for his workers, a sawmill, gristmill, company store, farms, ore railroad, three furnace stacks (including an anthracite coke stack), and more than 11,000 acres of land.

By 1903 the furnace ceased to operate, although ore was taken out of this area until 1912. What is left on the northern side of this "company town" is the furnace and an early nineteenth-century double log house, which is preserved by the Catoctin Furnace Historical Society and used as a museum and interpretive center.

For additional information, write to the Catoctin Furnace Historical Society, Thurmont 21788, or call Cunningham Falls State Park, (301) 271–7574. The furnace, remaining houses in Catoctin Village, and Harriet Chapel can be seen along Route 806, on the east side of Route 15, about 12 miles north of Frederick.

The *Frederick News Post* offers day and night tours through the newspaper office for adults and children as young as four or five. The tour lasts about forty-five minutes and goes through the editorial, advertising, circulation, and press rooms, and it provides an explanation about how a paper is written and printed. At night, Ed Waters gives the tours; during the day it is Mike Powell. They like to have about two weeks' notice and prefer not more than twenty to a group.

You might notice that the building does not seem to connect properly in the middle, and you would be right. Stand back from the front facade and notice that the front door has been filled in; this used to be a trolley barn, and the trolleys would go through the middle of the buildings on either side of this central portion. You can tell from the way the floor goes up and down with almost no rhyme or reason that it was put together after the fact. Sorry, but the trolley tracks have been removed.

For tour reservations or information, contact the *Frederick News Post*, 200 East Patrick Street, Frederick 21701 (301–662–1177).

A word about churches in Frederick. There are eleven of note, including one synagogue, whose histories and architectural styles date from the colonial, revolutionary, and Civil War eras. Tours are available during the year, and a brochure is available from Frederick tourism that details the history of each house of worship. A special time for all the churches is the Candlelight Tour held in December. Each church is decorated for the holiday, and hosts are on hand to greet visitors and answer questions. Special music and presentations are provided at various churches throughout the evening and free parking is available. Hospitality rooms are located at a number of places, and the one at Trunk Hall in the Evangelical Lutheran Church is handicapped accessible.

Many prominent Marylanders now reside in **Mount Olivet Cemetery**, including Francis Scott Key, Barbara Fritchie, Governor Thomas Johnson, along with veterans of the American Revolution, the Civil War (over 800 Confederate soldiers), World War II and more than 25,000 other people.

A statue of Key stands over 9 feet tall on a monument that is 15 feet high and 45 feet around; you can't miss the statue because it welcomes you at the main entrance. The United States flag standing by him flies twenty-four hours a day in honor of his writing the lyrics to "The Star-Spangled Banner."

Much of the money collected for the $25,000 monument was donated in dimes and dollars by people all over the country.

Little green and white signs direct you to the graves of Governor Johnson and Barbara Fritchie, who are sort of across the road from each other. Johnson was a revolutionary patriot, born in Frederick County in 1732 (the same year as George Washington), and was a prominent member of the Continental Congress. He was the first governor of the state of Maryland and associate justice of the United States Supreme Court.

Fritchie was made immortal by John Greenleaf Whittier's poem about her bravery against General Stonewall Jackson, when she flew the Union flag and dared soldiers to "Shoot if you must, this old gray head, but spare your country's flag." A monument of Maryland granite with the Whittier poem on a bronze table was unveiled on September 9, 1914.

The cemetery is considered one of the most beautiful and distinguished in this part of the country. The address is Mount Olivet Cemetery, South Broadway, Frederick.

There are numerous **campgrounds** where you can spend a night or two, and Frederick is close enough to Washington and Baltimore to be used as a base, if you wish.

Two of the better-known private campgrounds are Ole Mink Farm ("wilderness camping in comfort") and Crow's Nest Lodge Campground (both are near Thurmont).

Ole Mink Farm, owned and operated by Pat and Gordon Irons and Debbie and Mike Irons, offers large, secluded campsites, many with electricity and water, on a daily, weekly, or monthly basis. They have heated rest rooms with hot showers, a swimming pool, stocked fishing pond, mountain trout stream, play area, indoor game room, camp store, hiking trails, firewood, dump station, and worship service. Cabins are available, including one heated by passive solar energy. Each cabin accommodates a maximum of two couples or a family of two adults and three children. Kitchens are fully equipped, but you must provide the linens. Pets are not allowed. You can write to the Irons at 12806 Mink Farm Road, Thurmont 21788, or call (301) 271–2204 or 271–7012.

Crow's Nest Lodge Campground, owned and operated by Ned and Renna Haynes, has 110 campsites located along Big Hunting Creek, a mountain trout stream that flows through the Catoctin Mountains. Each spacious campsite is designed to accommodate a large tent, tent trailer, or travel trailer. Most of the sites are shaded, and many have water and electricity.

At the campground are a spring-fed, fresh-water pond for swimming and wading, 10 miles of scenic foot trails that wind through the Catoctin Mountain park, fishing, nature study, and a half-dozen action sports. Pets are welcome, as long as they are on a leash at all times. The address is Crow's Nest Lodge Campground, P.O. Box 145, Thurmont 21788, or call (301) 271–7632.

As mentioned in Washington County, several crafters have banded together to create the Valley Craft Network. One of the members is the Catoctin Pottery, owned by Susan and John Hanson who are the only network members in Frederick County.

The Hansons make handmade stoneware and porcelain in an 1810 water-powered gristmill on Catoctin Creek. Lewis Mill is a prime example of the adaptive use of a historic structure; the mill is meticulously reconstructed and houses a modern living space, studio, and retail showroom. Preservation of the environment is demonstrated by the use of solar heat and a waterless composting toilet.

In the studio showroom are works in clay, such as tableware, table and swag lamps, ceramic art, wall plaques, and tiles. Commissions are accepted.

Also on display at the pottery are handcrafted leather goods by Artie Rosati. You can reach him at P.O. Box 162, Highway 17, Middletown 21769 (301–371–5856).

Catoctin Pottery is open Monday through Saturday, 10:00 A.M. to 5:00 P.M., and is located on Poffenberger Road, off Old Middletown Road, Jefferson 21755 (301–731–4274).

For additional tourism information, write to the Executive Director, Tourism Council of Frederick County, 19 East Church Street, Frederick 21701, or call (301) 663–8687.

Montgomery County

Long-time area residents (anyone who's been here for more than ten years) will remember the awkward, sprawling image of the Bethesda intersection of Wisconsin Avenue, Old Georgetown Road, and East-West Highway. Personally, we remember it from when we used to hang out at the Hot Shoppes restaurant on Saturdays after high school football games between arch-rivals Montgomery Blair and Bethesda Chevy Chase (B-CC). (Go, Blazers!)

The presence at this intersection of the **Pioneer Lady Statue**, or Madonna of the Trail, symbolizes the importance of these roads even in their early days. Harry Truman dedicated the statue on April 19, 1929, in honor of the pioneer spirit and the National Pike, which connected the country from this spot on the East Coast to the town of Upland, California on the West Coast.

This was the twelfth of twelve statues to be installed; the other statues were erected (chronologically) in Springfield, Ohio; Wheeling, West Virginia; Council Grove, Kansas; Lexington, Missouri; Lamar, Colorado; Albuquerque, New Mexico; Springerville, Arizona; Vandalia, Illinois; Richmond, Indiana; Washington, Pennsylvania; and Upland, California.

The memorial (which faces east, whereas most of them face west) is dedicated to the pioneer mothers of the covered-wagon days. The engraving reads: "Over this highway marched the army of Major General Edward Braddock, April 14, 1755 on its way to Fort Duquesne," and "[This is] the first military road in America, beginning at Rock Creek and Potomac River, Georgetown, Maryland, leading our pioneers across the continent to the Pacific." The Pioneer Lady statue is located between the post office and the Hyatt Regency Hotel at the corner of Wisconsin Avenue, East-West Highway, and Old Georgetown Road in Bethesda.

When the statue was reinstalled in 1986, after years in storage due to subway and hotel construction, it was the first in a collection of perhaps twenty-five commissioned works by visual artists to be installed along Bethesda's streets. Known as the Bethesda Urban District, this area has more than 130 restaurants, from traditional to trendy, from down-home to deluxe. One of these is the Benihana in the Airrights Building, which is one of the oldest restaurants in the district and, when it opened in 1974, was only the sixteenth in the Benihana chain.

Downtown Silver Spring also has changed drastically and

will continue to do so as the metro has an influence on working and traveling patterns. Even if you do not use the metro system to travel into Washington, stop by the Silver Spring station.

A mural, 100 feet long and 8 feet high, was installed as part of the MetroArt I arts project (see also Prince George's County). Created by Sally Callmer of Bethesda, who previously was a miniaturist, the **Penguin Rush Hour Mural** was meant as a temporary installation but has become such an integral part of the community that the Montgomery County Department of Transportation has purchased the twenty-five panels to be a permanent fixture. It brings life to a previously drab area, and because of the lighting, it is the brightest single point in that downtown area. The idea for the penguin signs advocating ride sharing and use of the Metro came from this mural.

Montgomery's Forest Glen Metro station, which is nearly 200 feet below ground level, is the deepest in the system and maybe in the world. The Wheaton escalator, at more than 228 feet, is the metro system's longest escalator.

While you are in Silver Spring, drive by the Silver Spring Acorn. It is easy to spot this little park, located near the spring from which the area received its name, with its gazebo shaped by pillars and a "hat" with the configuration of an acorn. Benches are provided for a lunch break or a moment of rest. Francis Preston Blair—a wealthy and prominent eighteenth-century landowner, power broker, newspaper owner, and member of President Jackson's Kitchen Cabinet—and his daughter were out riding one day when they found this spring. The sunlight reflecting off the sand or mica in the bottom made the minerals look like silver, and this the name of his estate and the area, Silver Spring.

In 1942 the park was acquired by a local citizens group, and it was restored in 1955. Incidentally, the area, which is not incorporated, is called Silver Spring, not "springs," as in the Florida town. The Silver Spring Acorn is on Newell Road at the intersection of East-West Highway and Blair Mill Road, one block south of Georgia Avenue (across the street from the Canada Dry bottling plant).

Near the White Flint metro station is a large, upscale shopping center, White Flint Mall. The "Post Office of the Future," one of two such prototypes in the nation, opened here in September 1989. Designed to cater to busy people who have convenience on their minds, it is considered a cross between an airline ticket counter, a gift shop, and a video arcade. Computerized vending machines called Autoposts weigh packages, determine the cost for mailing, accept up to $20, and issue metered postage strips—all through a touchscreen computer. Infopost "talks" in English, Spanish, and French about postal services, mailing and delivery options, stamp collecting, and shop-by-mail services. If this works well, you may soon see one at your neighborhood mall.

Near the Takoma Park metro station are a number of boutiques, including Arise for ethnic and contemporary fashions; an agreeable bakery called Everyday Gourmet; Kaz department store, which is billed as the smallest department store in the world; and Now & Then, which specializes in cotton basics for women and children as well as restyled military and vintage items "for the whimsical, wacky and wearable."

On Saturdays during the spring-to-fall season, a block of Laurel Avenue is closed to vehicular traffic and becomes a farmer's market, which has people nearly clogging the subway system for early-morning selections. For more information write to Historic Takoma, P.O. Box 5781, Takoma Park 20912, or call (301) 585–3542.

Another farmer's market is located in Bethesda, just two or three blocks from the above-mentioned Pioneer Lady statue. This is the Montgomery Farm Woman's Cooperative Market, which was started during the depression. Its first sale date was set for February 4, 1932, and a second sale was held on April 20; it became so popular that they began traditional Wednesday and Saturday sale days. You can stop by the market and find all manner of food—including Pennsylvania Dutch double-baked ham and baked goods—and even rocking chairs and craft items, particularly during the winter. Our favorite stall is The Marquez Farm Stand in the back left-hand corner, as you walk in from Wisconsin Avenue. There Rick and Chun II Marquez, and sometimes their daughter, sell delectable pies, cakes, scones, Baltimore cheese bread, all-beef summer sausage, bratwurst, German salami, nitrite-

Silver Spring Acorn

free bacon, and other baked goods and meats. You can reach the Marquez family at (301) 530–9098.

The Montgomery Farm Woman's Market is at 7155 Wisconsin Avenue, Bethesda 20814. Market days are Wednesday and Saturday from 7:00 A.M. to 2:00 P.M. throughout the year.

Another view of the market is in the Bethesda **Post Office Mural** done by Robert Gates in 1939. This definitely represents a Montgomery County tradition, unlike the stereotypical transportation scene painted in the Towson Post Office. The Bethesda mural was restored in 1967 with funds provided by the Montgomery Farm Woman's Cooperative Market. The post office is at 7400 Wisconsin Avenue, Bethesda 20814.

Two other post office buildings in the area have murals. One is in Silver Spring and was painted in 1937 by Nicolai Cikovsky (of the Towson transportation mural incident); it's called "The Old Tavern," reflecting life in the area during and after the Antebellum period. The Old Post Office Building is at 8412 Georgia Avenue, Silver Spring 20901.

The other mural was done by New York artist Judson Smith in 1940 and is of "Sugar Loaf Mountain." Supposedly, it was painted from the porch of an estate called Inverness, which was built in 1818 by Benjamin White. The view includes fields and farm buildings, and it hangs over the wall where the lock boxes used to be located. Rockville Post Office is at 2 West Montgomery Avenue, Rockville 20850.

Speaking of the White family, **White's Ferry** is the only remaining ferry system on the Potomac River, connecting White's Ferry, Maryland to Leesburg, Virginia. It probably is more important these days than when it began operation in 1828, for it is the only river crossing between the American Legion Bridge on the Washington (or Capital) Beltway to the south and east, and the point of Rocks bridge to the north and west. Regular commuters and tourists can easily tell when there is a major backup on the beltway, because these back-country roads become filled with drivers escaping the jam.

The ferry *General Jubal Early* (named for a Confederate leader) runs the 1,000-foot crossing on a cable propelled by a diesel tug in about three minutes. It can hold eight cars and operates all year, weather and river conditions permit-

Montgomery Farm Woman's Cooperative Market

ting, on a demand basis. A sundries, souvenir, and country store is open on the Maryland side from spring through fall. The ferry slip is off Route 107. Call (301) 394–5200 for information.

Just up the ramp from White's Ferry landing is the ditch that was once the Chesapeake & Ohio Canal and is now the longest and thinnest national historical park in the country, narrowing to less than 50 feet at one point. There was a time when there were twenty trading posts along the 185-mile canal, which ran from Cumberland to Washington, D.C., roughly paralleling the Potomac River.

In 1988, conservationists spent three months clearing away foliage and found a 150-foot foundation of a nine-teenth-century depot and granary. From the Civil War until 1924, canal boats headed down to Washington, D.C., where they would tie up to a three-story wooden storage building called the Granary to load up with grain from area farms. In the sixty years since the canal closed, the Granary and canal have been neglected and overgrown by trees and shrubbery.

When you tell someone you're going to **Roy's Place,** they think you're talking about that old cowboy movie star. But this Roy's Place is in Gaithersburg, and it is far from fast food and fast eating. In fact, the menu tells you that if you are in a hurry, go someplace else. No, it is not fine dining. It is just sandwiches, and more sandwiches—some of the weirdest sandwiches you've ever imagined.

How would you like a sandwich with roast beef, fried oys-ters, and a side serving of tartar sauce? Would you prefer provolone cheese, anchovies, blue cheese dressing, onions, and lettuce? The menu features some 170 different sand-wiches, or you can start at the front page with a salad selec-tion and skip to the back page for a simple hamburger, if you do not feel like reading the equivalent of a novella before you eat.

Roy's has been open since 1971, and several local and national celebrities have had sandwiches named after them. The decor is just as interesting and off-beat as the menu, with posters, old advertisements, and a sign by the skylight that says THIS WAY OUT.

Roy's Place is at 2 East Diamond Avenue, Gaithersburg (301–948–5548). Hours are Monday through Thursday 11:00

A.M. to 11:00 P.M.; Friday and Saturday 11:00 A.M. to midnight; and Sunday 12:00 noon to 11:00 P.M. No reservations are accepted.

The **Olney Theatre** opened in 1942 as a stop on the summer "straw-hat" circuit, closed because of the war, and then reopened in 1946 with Helen Hayes starring in *Good Housekeeping.* Other luminaries who have graced its stage include Tallulah Bankhead, Gloria Swanson, and Bea Lillie. The late Reverend Gilbert Hartke, head of Catholic University's drama department, took over the management in 1953, providing exposure for his students as well as Carol Channing, John McGiver, and Frances Sternhagen. Bill Graham is now managing director and James D. Waring is artistic director.

Known as the State Summer Theatre of Maryland, Olney Theatre started a new tradition in 1989 with the annual production of *The Butterfingers Angel, Mary & Joseph, Herod the Nut*, and the *Slaughter of 12 Hit Carols in a Pear Tree*, a Christmas entertainment by noted playwright William Gibson. The theatre also is known for the elected officials it attracts, particularly on opening night, both to see the outstanding presentations and to be seen.

The Victorian farmhouse next door (circa 1880) is the Actors' Residence, and housing is provided for the cast in season. Actually two casts stay there at one time, one for the show in production and one for the show in rehearsal. On opening night post-performance festivities take place here.

The mailing address for Olney Theatre is P.O. Box 550, 2001 Route 108, Olney 20832; their phone number is (301) 924–3400.

After a day of sightseeing, you have a choice of two evening entertainments, and they are the **Burn Brae Dinner Theatre** in Burtonsville and the Harlequin Dinner Theatre in Rockville.

Burn Brae was the first dinner theater in the Washington area (opened in 1968), and they have continued to provide outstanding entertainment. At times they present a full-blown production with a huge cast, such as *Joseph and the Amazing Technicolor Dreamcoat* or *Evita,* and at other times they have a small, intimate play such as *I Do! I Do!* They may even have a pre-show tabletop magician or a weekly children's magic show.

With each show there is a menu change, but a typical buffet might consist of seventeen items, including salad, fish, roast beef, honey-basted Virginia ham, pasta primavera, chicken, meatballs, hot vegetables, homemade bread and muffins, and desserts.

When Burn Brae opened in an unused dressing room of a community pool in 1968, little did Bernie Levin and John Kinnamon realize they were starting a terrific tradition. Today the Washington area is the home of the largest number of dinner theaters in the country. Because there are so many of them, they foster a group of performers who know they will receive excellent training as well as be seen by the many talent scouts who come through this area.

Burn Brae Dinner Theatre is at 15029 Blackburn Road, Burtonsville 20866; call (301) 792–0290 or 384–5800.

Large, lavish productions are the hallmark of the **Harlequin Dinner Theatre.** Whether it is the adorable *My One and Only* or the spectacular *La Cage Aux Folles*, the Harlequin surely will please with their dedication to perfection. Producer Nicholas Howey and business manager Ken Gentry have repeatedly told us how they spend at least two hours in rehearsal for every minute on the stage, and sometimes much more.

The buffet dinner is always a pleasant experience, with fresh vegetables in season, steamship round, chicken, fish, and much more. Friday night shows often are followed by a complimentary post-show cabaret, when the evening's stars come out to perform.

A nice bonus about the Harlequin is their production companies that visit cities all over the country, with shows such as *Gigi* with Louis Jordan in the lead. The Harlequin Dinner Theatre is at 1330 Gude Drive, Rockville 20850; call (301) 340–8515.

For additional tourism information, write to Karen Lentz, Executive Director, Conference and Visitors Bureau of Montgomery County, 401 Hungerford Drive, First Floor, Rockville 20850, or call (301) 588–8687 or 424–1740.

Prince George's County

More people hear of Prince George's County in the news than they realize. A sports event is broadcast from the Capital Centre in Largo; a marriage is performed on the old wooden roller coaster at the Wild World theme park outside of Kettering; someone inquires into the status of the Enola Gay restoration at the Paul E. Garber Facility in Silver Hill (part of the National Air and Space Museum, Smithsonian Institution); space flight information is reported from the Goddard Space Flight Center (and Museum) in Greenbelt where the hub of all NASA tracking activities takes place; or the president arrives at Andrews Air Force Base, the home base for Air Force One. Of course, Prince George's County is rarely mentioned, but all of this commerce, sport, and history is taking place here on a day-to-day basis.

Prince George's County is a place of "firsts" and "lasts." In the latter category is the Bladensburg Dueling Grounds, a small, wooden glen in the northeastern corner of Fort Lincoln Cemetery, adjacent to Colmar Manor. It was a court of last resort for nearly fifty years for offended gentlemen and politicians, who faced each other at ten paces with pistols and muskets. As noted on the historical marker placed by the Maryland–National Capital Park and Planning Commission:

> One of the most famous was that between Commodores Stephen Decatur and James Barron which was settled here on March 22, 1820. Commodore Decatur, who had gained fame as the conqueror of the Barbary pirates, was fatally wounded by his antagonist. Although Congress passed an anti-dueling law in 1839, duels continued here until just before the Civil War.

The dueling grounds are in the Anacostia River Park and near the intersection of Bladensburg Road and 38th Avenue in Bladensburg.

The College Park Airport is where the first military training in a military-owned airplane took place in October 1909. The plane was designed by Orville and Wilbur Wright. College

Park claims to being the "world's oldest continually operated airport," and today it is the only operating airport within the Capital Beltway. Pilots say they get a kick out of flying from the same airfield that the Wright Brothers used seventy-five years ago.

To those who think planned cities are new to the seventies or eighties, meet **Greenbelt**, a "first" in the arena of planned cities that was started in the thirties. From its inception, Greenbelt had a sense of history about it. It has been chronicled, catalogued, dissected, scrutinized, and studied many times over in thorough detail. Although its greenbelt has been gnawed away a little and the town is surrounded by town-house communities for Washington commuters, you still can see the core of the town, its Art Deco architecture, and its attempts to retain its identity.

Greenbelt is one of three planned greenbelt towns that were to be satellite towns on the edge of larger urban cores (the other two are Greenhills, Ohio, and Greendale, Wisconsin, outside of Cincinnati and Milwaukee respectively). The town was built with everything centered around an inner core, allowing residents to walk everywhere they had to go on pedestrian paths so that people would not have to intermingle with cars.

The town was superorganized and highly democratic, and residents met to discuss everything. (In fact, at one point they met to declare a moratorium on meetings.) A 1938 survey of the first residents indicated that the first amenities they wanted were a library and a public swimming pool. Maryland's first municipal pool opened in Greenbelt on Memorial Day 1939. As intimated, much of Greenbelt was constructed in an Art Deco style, and that includes the bathhouse, although some of the deteriorated brick has been replaced with aluminum siding. The library came in June 1939, and now the Rexford Guy Tugwell room honors the former Resettlement Administration chief, whose interest in the "garden cities" movement led to the development of these towns. Most likely every word that has been written about Greenbelt is contained in this room.

Greenbelt is at the northwest corner of the intersection of the Baltimore-Washington Parkway (Interstate 295) and the Capital Beltway (Interstate 495).

Special library collections, such as the Tugwell Room in Greenbelt, are not the exception in Prince George's County. As the Belair Estate in Bowie claimed to be the "Cradle of American Racing," it seems entirely appropriate that the Bowie Library has the Selima Room, with its extensive collection of horse racing records and materials. Selima was one of the original mares who started the bloodline of almost every racehorse in this country.

Other special collections in the Prince George's County library system include the Sojourner Truth Room, in the Oxon Hill branch; the Kerlan Room children's collection in the Hyattsville branch; and the Documents Library in the County Administration Building in Upper Marlboro, which appears to have every document pertaining to Prince George's County that was ever printed or penned.

The performing and visual arts are important in this county; although highly populated with Washington and Baltimore commuters, the area still is nearly 50 percent rural in its orientation. The Montpelier Center in Laurel is noted for its visual arts. Visual and performing arts options at the University of Maryland are nearly limitless, and the International Piano competition always draws an extraordinary crowd.

Also, after four years of planning and building, the county officially opened the doors to a new fine arts facility at Harmony Hall Regional Center in September 1989. Responding to the county's need for a professional music space and additional visual arts programs in the south portion of the county, the vacant Harmony Hall Elementary School was renovated to include the 210-seat John Addison Concert Hall, a lobby, and a gallery space. An infrared radio system was included to assist the hearing impaired. The school's former garden atrium and two classrooms were removed for the concert hall and lobby, and an interior wall between two other adjacent classrooms was removed to allow for a large exhibition space on the building's ground floor. On the second floor two more classrooms were combined to provide for a professional dance studio. For information on upcoming programs and exhibits write to the Harmony Hall Regional Center, 10701 Livingston Road, Fort Washington 20744, or call (301) 292–8331.

Several years ago the arts organizations of the Prince

George's and Montgomery counties in Maryland, northern Virginia, and Washington, D.C., agreed to promote a MetroArts contest for public art to be displayed in subway stations throughout the system. It was very successful, and a number of artists had works displayed at several metro stations, such as New Carrollton, for a year. A second contest, this one with prize money totalling $100,000, has been held, and installations are taking place. New Carrollton again has been selected to have a three-dimensional artwork, which will be on display for two years.

See the Montgomery County section, Silver Spring metro station, for details on the mural placed there, which has been purchased for permanent installation.

If you like murals as much as we do, you will be curious about Prince George's County's **Post Office Murals.** The one in Laurel of the "Mail Coach at Laurel," done by Mitchell Jamieson in 1939, reportedly was taken down during some General Services Administration restoration of the building and has not been returned since.

The mural in Upper Marlboro belies the theory that the painters should paint about the area, because this "Tobacco Cutters" done by Mitchell Jamieson in 1938 is indeed of tobacco, but, the locals say, it's a tobacco not grown in this state. The mural depicts the Virginia/North Carolina method of harvesting rather than the Maryland method.

Eugene Kingman, a noted muralist, painter, and museum director, created the five panels in the Hyattsville Post Office in 1938, jointly entitled "Hyattsville Countryside." He was born in 1909 and went to Yale University's College of Fine Arts and received an honorary Ph.D. from Creighton University. His work is in the Library of Congress collection and at the Philbrook in Tulsa, Oklahoma, among many other places. He also created post office murals in Wyoming, Rhode Island, and the lobby of the New York Times Building in New York City.

The Hyattsville murals depict the working man in heroic proportions. They reflect the remains of the agricultural and pastoral quality of the Hyattsville life-style that still existed in 1937 when Kingman used such muralist techniques as stylized horses, foreshortening, and a decorative cornstalk border.

The Hyattsville Post Office is at 4325 Gallatin Street, Hyattsville 20781. Call (301) 669–8905.

Understanding that Prince George's County was and still is a very agrarian county, you will appreciate the work of W. Henry DuVall. A life-long Prince Georgean, DuVall had the foresight to save tools from the nineteenth century, whether it was a scythe, froe, niddy-noddy, can opener, carpenter's plane, or foot-operated dental drill. This was the beginning of the **DuVall Tool Collection.** There is even a white building block that is blackened on one side, which apparently was obtained during a nineteenth-century architectural revision of the White House. The dark stains are said to be soot from the burning of the building during the War of 1812.

The Maryland National Capital Park and Planning Commission had the foresight to buy the agglomeration so that it would not be lost to the twentieth or twenty-first century. His collection, which was started in the 1930s, had more than 1,200 items by the time he died in 1979. More tools are accepted, so if you have something tucked away in your attic or out in the garage someplace—particularly if it is unique to Southern Maryland history—donate it here instead of to the dump.

You can return to yesteryear by viewing the DuVall Tool Collection, located in the Patuxent River Park, Sunday from 1:00 to 4:00 P.M. and by appointment. The address is 16000 Croom Airport Road, Upper Marlboro 20772. Call (301) 672–6074.

Poultry is a big part of the Eastern Shore's economy; so it might not make sense that there is a **Poultry Hall of Fame** in Beltsville. It was here, however, that the big-breasted Beltsville turkey you enjoy so much at Thanksgiving was created; thus its originator, Dr. T. C. Byerly, is honored here. Five poultry greats are inducted into this society every year.

Actually, Beltsville is the Department of Agriculture's largest research center, and the tour is fascinating. A visitor's center, in Building 186 (East), is open daily from 9:00 A.M. to 4:00 P.M. Guided tours are available by appointment. Call (301) 344–2403, or 344–2483. The mailing address is United States Department of Agriculture, National Agriculture Library, Second Floor, 10301 Baltimore-Washington Boulevard, Beltsville 20705. There is no admission charge.

There is other wildlife occupying the minds of specialists in Prince George's County. Situated on 4,700 acres, the **Patuxent Wildlife Research Center** specializes in research on endangered species, migratory birds, and environmental contaminants.

Established in 1839 as America's first national wildlife experiment station, it is charged with protecting and conserving the nation's wildlife and their habitats through research and critical debate. Throughout the years, the center has been involved in history-making discoveries, including the detrimental effects of DDT. Rachel Carson did most of her research here while writing *Silent Spring.*

Currently, the center is working to save the endangered whooping crane, California condor, Mississippi sandhill crane, and masked bobwhite; they have completed their successful program of repopulating America's proud symbol, the bald eagle. Scientists from more than fifteen countries conduct research at the center on a regular basis.

Patuxent is the largest wildlife research center in the world, and its visitor's center, when completed, will have a mission to "educate the public, especially students, about wildlife conservation on a global perspective." Until the visitor's center is open, you can drive through by yourself, staying on the paved road, or call Nell Baldachinno (301–498–0331 or –0300) at least several days in advance for a tour.

The Center and the National Fund for the Patuxent Wildlife Research Center were featured on a December 1989, "CBS Sunday Morning," program with Charles Kuralt. The Fund is a special committee of the Prince George's County Parks and Recreation Foundation, which facilitates a public/private partnership to raise funds on a national basis for the multi-million dollar National Wildlife Visitors Center.

The Patuxent Wildlife Research Center is located at Route 197 and Powder Mill Road, Laurel 20708 (301–464–6706). Contributions may be sent to PGCPRF, 13022 8th Street, Bowie 20715.

There are a few trendy eateries, a few fern bars, and any number of college hangouts in Prince George's County. Also, there are a few fine old traditional restaurants, particularly the Oakland Inn on Marlboro Pike in District Heights, the Old

Calvert House in College Park, and Chef's Secret in Greenbelt.

Our favorite restaurant in the county is probably the **China Pearl** in Greenbelt. Eric C. C. Lin is the managing partner of this Chinese-Indonesian establishment, which seats 150 people but still has an intimate feeling. The panorama of picture windows makes the nearby shopping center look almost glamorous in the evening lights. Nasi Goreng is a fried rice dish that is richer than Chinese fried rice and has more variety in its mixture, which includes chicken, beef, shrimp, garlic, fried shallots, cucumber, and a slightly sweet soy sauce. The Satay is delectable and has a peanut sauce that is not as pungent as that used in Thai restaurants. You can order the Satay in chicken, beef, or pork. Chow mein is available here, but it isn't on the menu.

When you visit the China Pearl, talk with Mr. Lin, and feel free to discuss atmospheric physics (he studied at Peking University), opera, his travels through southern China and Hong Kong, or his former Cleveland Park restaurant, the Happy Inn. But go to enjoy his marvelous food and gracious hospitality.

The China Pearl, 7701 Greenbelt Road, Greenbelt 20770, is open Sunday through Thursday 11:30 A.M. to 10:00 P.M. and Friday and Saturday 11:30 A.M. to 10:30 P.M. Call (301) 441–8880.

Another fine restaurant is located in a quaint and historic home, the **Mount Airy Plantation.** On the National Register of Historic Landmarks, it was a hunting lodge for the lords Baltimore in the 1600s. Later it became a working plantation, and George Washington's stepson was married in this house. It is owned by the state and leased out as a restaurant and inn.

A nearly mile-long serpentine drive, sprinkled with ground-level lighting, winds through stately trees leading to the manor house, which is lovingly restored to its eighteenth-century appearance (with a few twentieth-century additions to bring things up to date). Inside, there is a skylight roof for sun and stars, period furnishings, antiques, mural wallpapers from a New York museum in the dining room, wooden floors with Oriental carpets, oil paintings, and fine linens over the tablecloths, which are set with splendid china.

Chef Janet Terry, a well-known chef in Washington, D.C., (at Samplings, West End Cafe, and Aux Beaux Champs at the Four Seasons in Georgetown) will satisfy your palate with seasonal fare and products from the plantation's working colonial garden.

Twelve suites are available after your evening's repast, or a late dip in the swimming pool, or even a brisk game or two on the tennis court. Perhaps you would prefer a visit to the two formal gardens, one of which is a Punging garden (a Chinese version of a Bonsai garden).

Michael Such is general manager and partner in this operation, which he and the partners hope will be the first of many historic inns they operate.

Dinner, with gratuities and a glass of wine, should cost about $45. An overnight suite with fireplace, including breakfast, should run between $125 and $175. Because it is so close to Washington and its suburbs, Mount Airy should be a perfect getaway, for a weekend or any day of the week.

Mount Airy Plantation, 8714 Rosaryville Road (⁹⁄₁₀ mile west of Route 301) is in Upper Marlboro. They are open for dinner from 6:00 to 9:00 P.M. Tuesday through Saturday; on Sunday they serve brunch from 12:00 noon to 2:30 P.M. and dinner from 5:00 to 9:00 P.M. Call (301) 856–1860 for reservations. The restaurant is handicapped accessible, and there is valet parking.

Dinner of a different sort is available at **Petrucci's Dinner Theatre** in Laurel. If this building looks like an old movie theatre, that's because it is. It was saved from obscurity, the wrecking ball, and X-rated movies by the Petrucci family. Now there is sprightly entertainment such as *Greater Tuna* and *Broadway Bound,* and the effulgent Larry Shue play *The Foreigner.* Italian dishes highlight the menu.

Petrucci's Dinner Theatre is at 312 Main Street, Laurel 20707. For reservations call (301) 725–5226.

Last, but not least, is the covered bridge in Bowie. It's located at the Bowie Race Course, which is now an equestrian center rather than a racetrack. Alas, the bridge is for horses moving from the stables to the track for their workouts, not for people or cars. It is almost brand new—construction was completed in 1988—making it perhaps the only covered bridge to have been built in this country for decades.

For additional tourism information, write to J. Matthew Neitzey, Executive Director, Prince George's Travel Promotion Council, 8903 Presidential Parkway, Suite 201, Upper Marlboro 20772, or call (301) 967–8687.

Off the Beaten Path in Southern Maryland

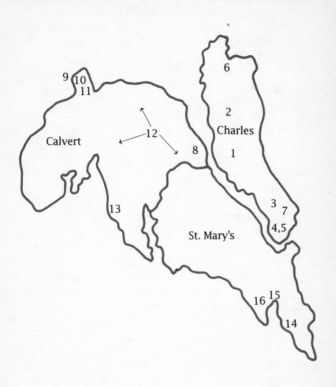

1. Country Peddler of Calvert County
2. The Wright Touch
3. Vera's White Sands
4. Calvert Marine Museum
5. Solomon's Pier
6. Penwick House
7. Flag Ponds Nature Park
8. Benedict
9. Marshall Hall
10. Mount Carmel Monastery
11. Friendship House
12. Tobacco Auctions
13. Pope's Creek
14. Freedom of Conscience Statue
15. Farmer's market
16. Toddy Hall Pottery

Southern Maryland

Parts of Charles, Calvert (pronounced Culvert by the locals), and St. Mary's counties probably have changed more because of avulsion and accretion than because of developmental encroachment since the first English colonists settled here in the mid-1600s.

With the more stringent wetlands restrictions recently imposed by our federal and state governments, it is possible that the Southern Maryland you see today will be the same as the one you see ten, twenty, thirty, or more years from now.

As you drive down these roads, you will see signs of those early settlements when brave men and women came seeking new lives, religious freedom, and adventure. Dozens of churches, some dating to the early eighteenth century, dot the historic landscape.

Although tobacco is apparently weakening in the marketplace, it is still in strong evidence here. You will not see any evidence of this labor-intensive crop in the spring, for it is very fragile and the seeds must be started in flats indoors and then individually transplanted outside in the summer. In the fall and early winter, you will see the barns with their air slats open to assist in drying the tobacco. Photographers come flocking to catch that picture-perfect moment when the plants are green and yellow and strongly contrast with the red-sided barns.

Water has made its influence felt, of course; there are many waterside communities, places to buy and eat fresh seafood, and aquatic research centers.

In Southern Maryland we looked for the markets that keep a community alive, and we found several community craft centers and talented artisans. We hope you will take time to enjoy the maritime influence and the fine and unusual dining surrounding, or perhaps surrounded by, this rich coastal area.

Calvert County

If you like country crafts, you'll find an abundance of them in Calvert County, for this is country, although it is being rapidly encroached upon by civilization. Here are two places to go for crafts where many artisans are represented.

Nearly two dozen local crafters show their work at the **Country Peddler of Calvert County**, a showcase for local talent including Janet Richardson, whose "Paws for Thought" collection includes stuffed animals; Nan Reid's crochet and knit items; Mary Rasmussen's counted cross-stitch needle-work and silhouettes; Owen Myers's canvas bags; Margaret Clark Smith's ceramics; Madie Winike's stained-glass pieces; and Virgie Finley's needlepoint. Also sold here are potpourri, home-grown luffas, and handmade brooms from the Calvert Homestead.

The Country Peddler is behind Bowens Grocery, where you can buy hand-cut meats, and across the street from the Bowens Garage Antique Center. The shop is open 10:00 A.M. to 5:00 P.M. Thursday, Friday, and Saturday; it is located parallel to Route 2-4, on Old Town Road, Route 524, Huntingtown 20639. Call (301) 257–3105.

Works from nationally recognized crafters can be found at **The Wright Touch**, owned and operated by sisters Sue Hill and Eve Wright. Tom Clark Woodspirits may be the biggest-selling items here, and Clark even stops by to talk with his fans. You can find handcrafted gifts, handwoven throws, country pine furniture, collectibles, decorating accessories, Christmas decorations, and Christmas curtains.

The Wright Touch is at 3150 Solomons Island Road, Route 4 southbound (turn at Gardner's Citgo station), Huntingtown 20639. Call (301) 535–5588. The shop is open Tuesday through Thursday 11:00 A.M. to 6:00 P.M.; Friday and Saturday 10:00 A.M. to 6:00 P.M.; and Sunday 12:00 noon to 5:00 P.M. Inquire about winter holiday hours and the antique Christmas festival.

While in the neighborhood, you can visit Barbara Burnett at her small Calvert Homestead barn, the "Home of the R & B Brand," by traveling south on Route 2-4 to Sixes Road (Route 506) and driving in about 3 miles. It will be on your right at 4555 Sixes Road, Prince Frederick. Call (301) 535–3786 for hours and information.

On the way there, you will pass the Battle Creek Cypress Swamp Sanctuary. This is the northernmost stand of bald cypress trees in the country. There is no Spanish moss hanging from these boughs or southern belles in hoop skirts; instead, there is a good interpretive center and a great place for nature photography in the spring and early summer when the blooms are most profuse. Bring fast film and a tripod, because the light is heavily filtered through the canopy.

By the way, those thick fuzzy vines climbing the trees along the boardwalk through the swamp are poison ivy and just as dangerous as the three shiny leaves if you are allergic. The sanctuary is on Grays Road off Sixes Road (Route 506). Call (301) 535–5327.

There are places called Hollywood and California in Maryland (both in St. Mary's County), and major motion pictures have been made in the state, but nothing equals **Vera's White Sands** restaurant. A summer pastime that should not be missed, Vera Freeman's restaurant is decorated with souvenirs from her worldwide travels.

Imagine you are Lauren Bacall, Humphrey Bogart, or Peter Lorre, or even Bob Hope, Bing Crosby, or Hedy Lamarr on the road to someplace; you would feel right at home here. What are your decorative tastes? Would you like banana trees, beaded room dividers, carved elephants inlaid with ivory, giant clamshells, and leopard-skin bar stools to provide the atmosphere? Bamboo and rattan are in every corner. Steam up the scene with a little romantic intrigue, and you do not have to travel far to find the exotic. The view overlooks the Patuxent River, and the meal will be a memorable one.

Vera's seafood specialty is bouillabaisse with shrimp, scallops, filet of fish, crab, clams, and mussels, served in a tomato and wine sauce.

Vera's White Sands is in Lusby on White Sands Drive. The restaurant opens about the end of April and closes mid-November, Tuesday through Saturday 5:00 to 9:00 P.M. and Sunday 1:00 to 9:00 P.M. Call (301) 586–1182.

Continuing south or southeast on Route 2-4, you will come to Solomons Island, which has a new visitor center that is open from spring through late fall. Across the street is the **Calvert Marine Museum,** and parking is behind the administration building.

The Calvert County Museum is proof that a museum can be fun, fascinating, and fact-filled. This museum has grown from a seed planted by LeRoy "Pepper" Langley in 1970, and it is certainly worth a visit for a number of reasons.

The first reason is the children's room. You have to be at least three years old to visit, since the exhibits include live animals. We were fascinated by the albino blue crab, although it may not be there when you visit since the exhibits change from time to time. We had never seen the likes of this crab before.

Also, there is a pile of earth with fossils from the Calvert Cliffs that you can dig in. It can be difficult, time consuming, and perhaps illegal to search for fossils at outdoor sites, but not here. One shark's tooth per person, please. This room is more fun than a bushel of crabs that has just been dusted with seasoning. Yet there is more, and you are on your own to enjoy, to be entertained, and to be educated. Even the more conventional exhibits about boating, the paleontology of Calvert Cliffs, and the estuarine biology of the Patuxent River and the Chesapeake Bay are well handled.

Next, go outside. There you will see three of the greatest nonedible treasures the Bay area has to offer. The first is the aforementioned "Pepper" Langley, who turned seventy-five in 1990. He is in semiretirement these days, which means he usually shows up only on Saturday and Sunday to help conduct woodcarving classes. He may be there at other times, however, because he seems to have trouble staying away from the museum.

When we last saw him he was working on a model of a saucy 1872 sidewheeler called the *St. Mary's*, which used to travel the Bay with freight and passengers. Pepper received his nickname in 1934 when he was busy stealing bases for his championship high school baseball team. Fellow teammates likened him to St. Louis Cardinals base-stealing whiz, Pepper Martin, and the nickname has stayed with him.

If our country declared people as national treasures like they do in Japan, "Pepper" Langley probably would be near the top of the list. His son Jimmy is now the head carver and created the scale model of Solomons Island that is in the museum.

Calvert's second treasure is the Drum Point Lighthouse, one of the old screw-pile, cottage-style lighthouses that used to protect the adventuresome watermen of the Bay. The two-story, hexagon-shaped structure was built in 1883 to mark the entrance of the Patuxent River. A crane and barge moved the stilted cottage to its current location in 1975. Take a few minutes to walk through the lighthouse (watch your head going up and down the steps) and mentally transport yourself to the time when people lived here and tended the light. It is romantic to think of the "good old days" when there were lightkeepers, but most of us don't think this remote life-style is very attractive these days.

By the way, the Cove Point Lighthouse is just north off the Route 2-4 highway. It is closed, but you can drive down the road and look at the light from this side of the fence, and if you are persistent you can call (301) 326–3254 to see if something is scheduled.

The third treasure is an old bugeye, the *William B. Tennison*, which takes people on cruises around the Bay. This bugeye is a Chesapeake Bay sailing craft built in 1988 at Crabb Island by B. P. and R. L. Miles. Her hull is "chunk built," or made of nine logs, rather than by a plank-and-frame method of construction. Originally rigged for sailing, she was converted to power in 1907, and a new, larger cabin was added aft.

You can cruise on the *Tennison* and see the Governor Johnson Bridge, the Solomons Island and Chesapeake Biological Laboratory, and the U.S. Naval Recreation Center at Point Patience. This is seeing the inner harbor and Patuxent River as you can never see them on land. Captain Rudy Bennett runs the one-hour cruise at 2:00 P.M. Wednesday through Sunday (minimum of ten people required) between May 1 and October 1, or you can charter the boat for your own event. Fares range from $3.50 per adult, $2.50 per child (5 to 12), or $12 per family (regardless of size) to $125.00 per hour for the charter. Call (301) 326–2042 for additional information.

The Calvert Marine Museum is open 10:00 A.M. to 5:00 P.M. Monday through Saturday and 12:00 noon to 5:00 P.M. on Sunday May through October; from November through April it is open 10:00 A.M. to 5:30 P.M. Monday through Friday and 12:00 noon to 4:30 P.M. on Saturday and Sunday. A wheelchair is available. Admission to the museum grounds, main exhibit building, and parking is free, although contributions and memberships are welcome. Admission to the lighthouse and the museum of the former J. C. Lore and Sons

Oyster House (½ mile down the street) is $1.00 for adults and $.50 for children under twelve. Children under five are free. You can contact the Calvert Marine Museum at P.O. Box 97, Solomons 20688, or call (301) 326–2042.

By the time you have finished exploring this museum and the oyster house annex, it surely will be time for lunch or dinner. You have your choice on Solomons Island, with John and Kathy Taylor's Tiki Bar serving the best-tasting food, and it is worth your time to stop by Edgar Woodburn's Pier 1 Restaurant and grocery store.

Solomon's Pier may offer the best view, particularly of the Governor Thomas Johnson Bridge and the water at sunset. While you wait for your meal to be served, you can take a look at the old pictures of the pier. During warm weather, there are tables on the deck for alfresco dining. During cooler months, you should try the waterman's stew, which has an assortment of fresh seafood and vegetables.

Take time to stop by the Tradewinds gift shop, adjacent to Solomon's Pier, for Solomons memorabilia, handmade gifts, decoys and woodcarvings, fresh bread and gourmet desserts, and the famous "wobble, wobble, quack, quack."

Solomon's Pier is at P.O. Box 376, Main Street, Solomons Island 20688. Call (301) 326–2424.

One of the better restaurants in several surrounding counties is the **Penwick House.** During the winter months, it is the perfect place to enjoy "the warmth of the fireside, a steaming mug of wassail, the romance of candlelight, and a sumptuous meal to please the palate." Spring afternoons by the windows overlooking the greening countryside are just as spectacular.

A second attraction here is The Shoppe at Penwick, which has live greens, garlands, wreaths, ornaments, silk flowers, baskets, and homespun table coverings, to name just a few of the crafts and gifts available. During the winter season Penwick sponsors a free Christmas Greens Show with decorations designed during craft demonstrations.

Penwick House is on Route 4 northbound, Dunkirk 20754. The phone number is (301) 855–5388 or 257–7077.

Contained within the 327-acre park known as **Flag Ponds Nature Park** are wooded uplands, ponds, swamps, freshwater marshes, sandy beaches, and part of Chesapeake Bay.

Here you can clearly see the difference between the uplands and the wetlands, between the Cliffs of Calvert and the Chesapeake Bay. Wildlife abounds, including fox, muskrat, otter, turkey, whitetail deer, and pileated woodpecker. Special facilities include 3 miles of gentle hiking trails, rare plants such as the blue flag iris (from which the park derives its name), pond observation decks, picnic sites, a beach, a fishing pier, and a visitor center with wildlife exhibits.

One building remains from what was once a thriving "pound net" fishery that supplied trout, croaker, and herring to the bustling Baltimore markets during the first half of this century.

From April 1 through October 1 there is a daily permit charge of $3 per vehicle or a season pass of $10 per vehicle. Advance reservations are requested for group use of the park. Guided tours and other educational opportunities are available by advance request. Beach parking for the handicapped is available.

The Flag Ponds Nature Park is open 10:00 A.M. to 6:00 P.M. from Memorial Day through Labor Day and the same hours on weekends only from October through May (no admission charge during the winter). Call (301) 535-5327 or 586-1477. Take Route 4 for 10 miles south of Prince Frederick and look for the nature park entrance on the left.

For additional information, write to Marilyn Manning, Tourism Director, Department of Economic Development, Calvert County Courthouse, Prince Frederick 20678; call (301) 535-4583 or 855-1880.

Charles County

Most of the usual tourist attractions in Charles County are centered around La Plata and Port Tobacco (one of the oldest communities on the East Coast). On the eastern and western "ends" of the county, however, there are two interesting views of early Charles County.

On the northeastern-most tip of Charles County is the town of **Benedict**, named for Benedict Leonard Calvert, the fourth lord Baltimore. It was a flourishing town at least three times. The first was a period between 1817 and 1937, when steamboats carrying freight and passengers stopped here on their way to and from Baltimore and ports on the Rappahannock and Potomac rivers. The second time was when slot machines were legal in the county and people came to gamble from as far north as New Jersey and New York. The third time was in 1988, when the Governor Thomas Johnson Bridge from Solomons to St. Mary's was closed. Ferries were put in service, but many people detoured to Benedict and used the Patuxent River Bridge.

Benedict is also notable as the landing site for 4,500 British troops in August 1814. Local historians say it is the only town on United States soil that has been invaded by foreign troops, for these were the troops who marched on to the nation's capital. The British troops returned to Benedict with their wounded, and two of their soldiers were buried at Old Fields Chapel cemetery in Hughesville. During the Civil War, Camp Stanton was established here for recruiting and training a black infantry to serve in the Union Army.

Today this waterside town, the most inland port on the Patuxent River, has a post office (Dolores Buick is the postmaster), which is also the paperback lending library, a restaurant or two, and some "boatels" for storing boats. Sue and Maurice Roach own the Benedict Pier Restaurant and Marina, and Chappelear's is owned by Francis and Katherine Chappelear (an old Benedict family), who harvest some of the oysters they serve and buy "peeler" crabs for their delectable "soft shells." Veer off to the right of Route 231, just before the bridge, if you are looking for dockside atmosphere.

On the northwestern tip is **Marshall Hall**, which for three-quarters of a century was an amusement park for the young, the young-at-heart, and young lovers from around the Washington, D.C. area. Originally Marshall Hall was a thriving eighteenth-century plantation owned by the William Marshall family. By 1725 Thomas Marshall had built a Georgian-style mansion and other outbuildings, including a pier that extended into the Potomac River in a direct line with the entrance road, dividing the plantation into two mirrored halves. It is said that George Washington visited here frequently from his home across the river at Mount Vernon.

Due to financial losses from the Civil War, the property was lost to the Marshall family in 1866. It passed through a number of owners before the Mount Vernon and Marshall Hall Steamboat Company bought the estate in 1895 to develop it into a Victorian amusement park with gardens, croquet and jousting greens, gazebos, and concession stands.

The amusement park was torn down in the 1920s to be replaced by a more modern park, the one we natives remember. An evening at Marshall Hall started with a boat ride down the Potomac, past Mount Vernon on the right, to Marshall Hall. A few hours of rides and games, and then it was a boat ride back to Washington.

Discussions are held regularly about doing something with this property, but at this time there are only memories of the amusement park and some remnants of the mansion. Three walls stand eerily silhouetted in a morning fog together with a brick outbuilding and the Marshall Family cemetery, a fenced burial ground of about twenty-four known graves, half of which date back to the 1700s. The view of Mount Vernon across the river is still there as well. Marshall Hall is open daily and admission is free. To reach Marshall Hall, take Route 210 about 12 miles south of the Capital Beltway to Route 227. Turn right and follow the road about 5 miles to its end. Marshall Hall will be on your right; a large parking lot and boat ramp will be on your left.

On the other (north) side of the Charles County/Prince George's County line is the National Colonial Farm that is open Tuesday through Sunday. Call (301) 283-2113.

In between these two historic spots is **Mount Carmel Monastery**, the first convent for religious women in colonial America, founded on October 15, 1790. It was started by four Carmelite nuns, three of whom—Ann, Ann Theresa, and Susan Mathews—along with Reverend Charles Neale were natives of Charles County. The group set up temporary quarters at Chandler's Hope, then owned by the Neale family. Father Neale donated 860 acres to the Carmelites for their monastery to be built. Two of the original convent buildings have been restored and are open to visitors during the summer season. The other buildings are still used as an active convent.

If you are driving in from Route 301 on Mitchell Road, Mt. Carmel Monastery is on the left about ½ mile past Charles County Community College on Mt. Carmel Road.

The monastery is open from 8:00 A.M. to 4:00 P.M. Mass is said daily at 7:15 A.M. and on Sunday at 8:00 A.M. Call (301) 934–1654.

Across from the monastery on Mitchell Road, on the Community College property, is **Friendship House**, one of the oldest homes in the county. This four-room, hall-and-parlor style house was built by William Dent in 1680 on the Nanjemoy Creek. In 1968 it was dismantled by the Historical Society of Charles County and moved to its current location. Openings have been left in the structure so visitors can view the seventeenth-century construction techniques.

Friendship is open for tours and a ten- to fifteen-minute slide presentation from 12:00 noon to 4:00 P.M. on Saturday and Sunday, May through September. Tours by appointment are available at other times. There is a nominal admission charge. Call (301) 934–2251, extension 610, for information on Friendship House from the Southern Maryland Studies Center at Charles County Community College.

In your travels through the county, you may see evidence of tobacco, the most important crop in this area for 300 years. It takes 250 man-hours to produce one acre of tobacco (less labor-intensive crops may take as little as four man-hours), and Maryland tobacco is air dried in a "stick" of loose leaf tobacco made up of individual leaves. In contrast, Virginia tobacco is flue cured by heat in three days. During the three- to six-month drying or curing process, the stick of tobacco will lose more than one and a half gallons of water.

Tobacco Auctions are held every spring at Hughesville, Waldorf, and La Plata, and visitors are welcome to watch the auctions and tour the warehouses. However, as tobacco is replaced with less labor-intensive crops and as urbanization encroaches into Charles County, fewer farmers are planting tobacco and the auctions have been reduced in number. If you will be here between mid-March and early May, auction schedules and directions can be had by calling the Farmer's Warehouse (301–274–3124); Hughesville Warehouse (301 274–3101); or Edelen Brothers Warehouse (301–934–2601).

Pope's Creek is the best place to go for crabs and a view of the Potomac River. The 3-mile drive down Pope's Creek Road is also a little history lesson, for it was along this route that John Wilkes Booth found refuge after assassinating Abraham Lincoln. Two historical markers denote his stopping point along Pope's Creek Road for three days and his departure point to get across the Potomac into Virginia. (Dr. Samuel A. Mudd's house, where Booth was treated, is farther north in the county on Route 232 south of Route 382. It is open for tours, with a $2 admission charge for adults, from March to November; call (301) 934-8464 or 743-3837).

Down at Pope's Creek are the shells of oysters eaten over the centuries, first by Charles County Indians, then by settlers, and today by travelers. These shells cover some thirty acres to a depth of 15 feet in some places. If you prefer eating crabs and oysters to looking at old shells, stop by Robertson's, Captain Billy's, or Pier 3 for some crabs served in a traditional style. The tables are covered with paper and piles of those tasty crabs; a pitcher of beer accompanies the feast. Here you can learn why Maryland is called the Land of Pleasant Living.

The old building on your right as you drive to the water is an old Rural Electrification Administration powerhouse with lovely arched windows reminiscent of the Palladian style.

The bridge across the Potomac, 3 miles downriver, is the Governor Harry W. Nice Bridge. It opened in 1940, replacing Laidlow's Ferry, and was the first crossing the Potomac River south of the nation's capital. The 1938 ground breaking was presided over by President Franklin D. Roosevelt. The bridge is 1.7 miles long and 135 feet above the water, and carries nearly four million vehicles yearly. Passenger cars pay a $.75 toll in either direction.

For additional tourism information, write to David Boggs, Public Information Officer, Charles County Government Building, P.O. Box B, La Plata 20646, or call (301) 645-0559 or 870-3000.

St. Mary's County

There are some counties in Maryland that are off the beaten path even when you are on their most-traveled roads. St. Mary's is one of them. There are many different attractions that draw thousands of people here each year, yet it remains primarily historic and underdeveloped. From the Naval Air Test and Evaluation Museum (connected with the Patuxent

Naval Air Base), to the Old Jail Museum, to the Point Lookout State Park with its terrific camping area and beaches, to the crafts at Cecil's Mill and Christmas Country Store, you can spend a good deal of time down here.

Historic St. Mary's City was the first proprietary colony in America and the first capital of Maryland. There are still numerous traces of colonial times, including Sotterley Mansion, an eighteenth-century working plantation overlooking the Patuxent River. St. Clements Island, where you can discover the Potomac River Museum, was the landing site for Maryland's first white settlers. Historical churches abound.

St. Mary's City is actually a small town—just St. Mary's College, a post office, Trinity Episcopal Church, and a cluster of museum buildings. Scant development and modernization has meant that St. Mary's is the only early English settlement that is relatively undisturbed; thus it is a favorite of archaeologists, who have uncovered millions of artifacts in a relatively short time.

Some of the oldest buildings have proven particularly rich. Tolle-Tabbs (1750) and Van Sweringen (1600s) are practically reconstructed. Others, like St. John's (1638) and the Leonard Calvert House (1635), have the original foundations exposed to view. Still others, such as Hicks (1720), are marked with signs. You can explore this haunt of archaeologists during the summer digs or see the results of fifty years of unearthing Maryland's past at several sites. Stop by the Visitors Center of Historic St. Mary's City adjacent to the campus for information on current digs and displays.

With more miles of shoreline than square miles of land and a college campus full of students, you know this has to be a good party town. One can study only so long. St. Mary's College was St. Mary's Female Seminary, and it is considered one of the best buys in education, with its excellent teacher-student ratio and small enrollment of about 1,300 students. And the Potomac and Patuxent rivers, the creeks, the streams, and the Chesapeake Bay are ideal for biology and marine science studies. But the Bay also makes this area ideal for sailing, so it is frequently invaded by sailors seeking a home port. The annual Governor's Cup Regatta is considered one of the ten best sailing parties of the year by national sailors. The water is also perfect for those interested in sailboarding. With St. Mary's mild winters, students can enjoy boating about six months out of the school year.

The **Freedom of Conscience Statue** at the entrance to the college was erected by the counties of Maryland and symbolizes the religious freedom on which the state was founded. In 1649 at the request of town officials from St. Mary's, a guarantee of freedom of conscience to all Christians (freedom of other religions came later) was enacted by the state legislature.

All is not water, water, everywhere, however; some of the area is devoted to truck and produce farms. One of the major enticements into St. Mary's County is the several farmer's markets with their Amish goods, produce, antiques, and curios. As with most farmer's markets, the earlier you arrive, the better the selection. One **farmer's market** is of special note.

St. Mary's City specializes in locally grown fruits and vegetables, honey, baked goods, seafood, and flowers and plants. The market is open 12:00 noon to 4:00 P.M. every day from July through October. You will find the market near the visitor's center on Rosecroft Road in St. Mary's City. Call (301) 475–4406 or –4481 for information.

We met potter Michael Olson at his **Toddy Hall Pottery** about fifteen years ago when we were researching our first article about St. Mary's County. As we recall, he was tired of the rat race of professional teaching and had "retired" to the quiet life of his relatives from St. Mary's County. One of his objectives had been to recreate the pottery of the early St. Mary's settlers, and his "St. Mary's" work is available. He also produces some "Colonial Williamsburg" pieces.

We stopped by his studio, loved his work, and bought a flower pot, although we have been known to kill plastic greenery. Toddy Hall Pottery thrives today, still focused on beauty and quality, and you can buy pitchers, cups, bowls, and other ceramics. Olson also is creating sculptures and paintings these days.

The address for Toddy Hall Pottery is P.O. Box 64, Cherryfield Road, Drayden 20630. Take Route 5 south through Leonardtown, turn south on Route 249 at Callaway, then east on Route 244 (the Drayden Road) at Valley Lee, and follow the signs. Call (301) 994–0947 for hours.

Freedom of Conscience Statue

The *Captain Tyler* is a ferryboat that carries up to 150 passengers and operates between Point Lookout and Smith Island between June 11 and September 30. The fare is $25 per person (you can take your bike for no charge), dinner included, and children are half fare. The one-hour-and-forty-minute ferry departs at 10:00 A.M.; the return ferry leaves the island at 4:00 P.M. For more information contact Tyler's Cruises, Rhodes Point 21858, or call (301) 425–2771.

For additional tourism information, write to Cindy Woodburn, St. Mary's County Tourism Coordinator, St. Mary's County Chamber of Commerce, Route 8, Box 1B, Mechanicsville 20659, or call (301) 884–5555.

Off the Beaten Path on The Upper Eastern Shore

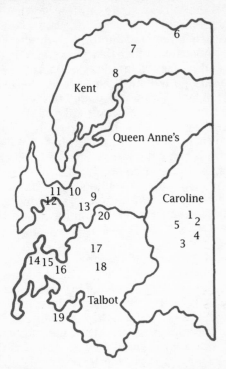

1. Caroline County Farmer's Market
2. Melvin House on the Green
3. Wye Oak Sculpture
4. Sophie Kerr House Bed and Breakfast
5. Ashly Acres
6. Livestock market
7. Kent Museum
8. Bicycle tours
9. Old Wye Grist Mill
10. Farmer's Market
11. Holly's Restaurant
12. Wildfowl Discovery Center
13. Orrell House and Bakery
14. Museum of Costume
15. St. Mary's Square Museum
16. Inn at Perry Cabin
17. Black & Decker
18. John S. McDaniel House Bed and Breakfast
19. Tred Avon Ferry
20. Wye Oak State Park

Upper Eastern Shore

On the eastern side of the Chesapeake Bay lies the Eastern Shore, a very distinct and separate entity from the "western shore." People here are dedicated to the ways of the watermen and to the riches the land can bring, although farming here means just about anything that grows except tobacco. At the eastern end of the William Preston Lane Jr. Memorial Chesapeake Bay Bridge is Kent Island, where the first European settlement in Maryland was founded in 1631. When the settlers came, they found the Nanticoke and Chop-tank tribes, who are now immortalized by some Indian lore exhibits and two rivers named after the tribes.

History surrounds the Bay's little towns and 500 sheltered harbors. The Bay is home to boatbuilders, sailors, fishermen (10,000 fishermen earn their livelihood from the Bay), and sportsmen. The waterways are often as secluded as in the days when pirates and buccaneers hid in the bays and inlets. Some say there may still be buried treasure stashed in the sand dunes.

Hunters flock here every fall, for this is a major stop for migrating birds on the Atlantic flyway. To conserve and protect those birds that are not so abundant, nearly $2 million has been raised for conservation projects along the flyway.

On the flat-as-a-pancake terrain, there are farmlands, stately manors, and, once again, small towns. It seems that most of Maryland is filled with small towns. And, fortunately, these towns are always sponsoring festivals celebrating the richness of the land or the sea.

Kent, Queen Anne's, Caroline, and Talbot counties offer many riches. We explore some farmer's markets, a livestock market, the remains of an oak tree, some eateries, a few bed and breakfast places, miniature horses that are not the ponies of Assateague and Chincoteague, bicycle tours to get you exploring the gentle countryside, a very old gristmill, a few museums, a factory tour, and the best biscuits you will ever have.

Caroline County

Caroline County is the only Eastern Shore county not directly on the ocean or the Bay, but there are calm waters, such as the Choptank River and Marshyhope Creek, state parks for canoeing and fishing, and an active crabbing and fishing industry. The prime interest here is agrarian, and the crops are bountiful. Corn, soybeans, cucumbers, tomatoes, peas, beans, sweet corn, cantaloupes, and melons fill the fields and make a stop at a local grocery store or fruit stand an essential part of anyone's visit.

The **Caroline County Farmer's Market**, in the county seat of Denton, is a fine place to find those locally grown products as well as some home-baked goods. The market is open from spring through autumn on Fridays from 11:00 A.M. to 3:00 P.M. It is located at Courthouse Green, Market Street, Denton.

While in the Denton area, you might want to stop by James and Mary Ellen Pelosky's place, the **Melvin House on the Green**, a fine dinner restaurant in Denton. Frequent menu changes feature fresh produce and seasonal favorites.

A late-fall menu at the Melvin House featured autumn lamb shanks braised with roasted peppers and eggplant, sauteed sea scallops with black bean sauce and spring onions, roasted ham served with honey-sweetened wild currants, poached northwest salmon garnished with ripened pears and leeks, and marinated flank steak with wild mushrooms and cured ham. A select wine list suggests an appropriate accompanying wine for each entree. This superb continental cuisine is served in a lovely Victorian setting.

Melvin House on the Green is at 106 Market Street, Denton 21629 (301–479–1513). Dinner is served Tuesday through Saturday from 5:30 P.M. A dress code is not enforced, but generally people come dressed up.

In June 1984, in the quiet hours of an early Sunday night, a thirty-five–ton limb from Maryland's state tree crashed to the ground. Being practical, the state decided that some of the limb should be made into souvenirs, such as gavels; but 70,000 pounds makes a lot of gavels.

The Maryland Forest, Park and Wildlife Service sent a two-ton chunk of wood to sculptor Steven Weitzman to create the **Wye Oak Sculpture.** He carved it into a monument in his shop at Seneca Creek State Park in Gaithersburg. On April 3, 1985, his sculpture of two children leaning over a shovel in the act of planting a tree was moved to its permanent home at Martinak State Park near Denton. The children, who are larger than life-size, are standing beneath a white oak tree in this 10-foot-tall statue that measures about 4½ feet from front to back.

Also at Martinak is the reconstructed hull of a wrecked pungy, a type of boat used on the Bay in the early nineteenth century. The park is open from sunrise to sunset daily except Christmas week. Martinak State Park is on Deep Shore Road, off Route 404, Denton; call (301) 479–1619.

The historical marker next to the Choptank Electric Cooperative on Routes 404 and 328, just west of Denton, marks the modest but historic Neck Meeting House. Built in 1802 by members of the Society of Friends, the meeting-house is believed to be the oldest house of worship in Caroline County. Most of the funds raised for the aluminum marker came from the recycling of aluminum cans by local residents. The Choptank Electric Cooperative is refurbishing the small building, and if you would like to look inside, stop by the cooperative for the key.

Cyclists love the house Sophie Kerr lived in during the late nineteenth century. It is now owned by Thelma and John Lyons, who operate it as the **Sophie Kerr House Bed and Breakfast**. Bikes are locked up in the barn at night, and a small workshop for bicycle repair is nearby.

Kerr wrote more than twenty-two novels and 500 short stories. She was managing editor of Woman's Home Companion from 1909 to 1919, and, most important to this book, she grew up in Denton.

The bed and breakfast, in the two-story frame house her parents occupied from the time it was built in 1861, features a smokehouse (now the honeymoon suite), the original big red barn, the original corn crib (now a playhouse with old-fashioned toys tossed about), and a newer enclosed swimming pool in back of the house. There are five guest rooms. Dinner is served on Limoges china with silverware and linen napkins, and coffee and cake are served nightly in front of the fireplace. Write to Sophie Kerr House,

Wye Oak Sculpture

Route 3, Box 7-B, Denton 21629, or call (301) 479–3421.

Ashly Acres produced the first miniature horses to participate in an inaugural parade—President Bush's. This nine-acre farm is owned by Robin Stallings, Karen Kilheffer, and Ashly Wayne Asbury, who breed, raise, and show quality registered miniature horses.

A miniature horse is a true horse, not a pony or a dwarf, and is very gentle. According to Ashly Acres, the ancestor of the modern miniature horse was first bred for the royal courts of Europe during the seventeenth century. They were often passed from one sovereign to another as diplomatic tokens of goodwill. When the power and wealth of the royalty began to decline, a few horses found their way into the traveling circuses of Europe. Some were used as pit ponies in the coal mines. The selective breeding process was interrupted, and the breed almost became extinct.

The American miniature horse is a scaled-down model of a full-sized horse, and can measure no more than 34 inches at the withers. Foals usually weigh between eighteen and twenty-five pounds and stand between 16 and 22 inches at birth. They come in all colors, and although they can be ridden by very small children, they usually are used in harness where they can easily pull a full-sized adult. They function best as lovable exotic pets.

In the early 1900s, a Virginian named Normal Fields imported some miniature horses with a shipment of pit ponies. He was so taken with them that he started a breeding program that continued for thirty-five years. Another Virginian, Smith McCoy, started with ten or twelve horses under 32 inches and built one of the largest miniature horse herds in the United States.

The address for Ashly Acres is R.D. 1, Box 207CC, Denton 21629. Tours for twenty-five people or more are available by appointment; call (301) 479–1159 to ask if you can join one.

For additional tourism information, write to Leigh Sands, Clerk, Caroline County Commissioners, P.O. Box 207, Denton 21629, or call (301) 479–0660.

Kent County

Kent County has the largest proportion of farmland to total acreage, yet it is bordered on the north by the Sassafras

River, on the south by the Chester River, and on the west by the Chesapeake Bay, so you can understand its multiple focal points. There might be an Old-Fashioned Fourth festival in Rock Hall, an Eastern Shore fish fry, and a Kent County Watermen's Association workboat race and docking course competition, all on the same summer weekend. After the harvest, it is time for goose and deer hunting.

For those who prefer architectural history to land and water sports, Chestertown, the county seat of the smallest county in the state, is said to be the tenth-favorite historic place in America because of the large number of restored eighteenth-century homes.

When driving through Kent County, it is wonderful to take time to see local sites, such as the Buck-Bacchus Store Museum; the picturesque view of waterfront homes at Chestertown; the Eastern Neck National Wildlife Refuge; the Geddes-Piper House (home of the legendary Mistress Kitty Knight), the 3,000-acre wildlife research and demonstration area known as Remington Farms; the Rock Hall Museum (Rock Hall is becoming more of a yachting center than the fishing center it used to be before the ban on catching the once-plentiful rockfish); and Washington College, the tenth-oldest college in this country, which George Washington helped to found.

For this book, however, we will stick with the people who live here today and how they make a livelihood. A weekly **livestock market**, dating back more than fifty years, is conducted by Harry Rudnick and Sons. It brings farmers from surrounding counties to Galena every Tuesday, fifty-two weeks a year, to bid on pigs and hogs at 1:30 P.M., calves at 2:45 P.M., and cattle at 4:00 P.M. This is not a dress-up event. There is no admission charge, and you can come as early as you like to watch the hands tag, weigh, and process the animals; then you can go into one of the two amphitheater rooms for the auction. The action all takes place down in the auction ring, at the bottom of the seats. Note that the seats are large steps, like at a high school football stadium, so if you need some artificial cushion to make you comfortable, remember to bring it along.

On the second and fourth Saturdays of the month, they auction antiques, furniture, glass, china, oriental rugs, and almost everything else anyone wants to sell. Frank Rudnick, the son of the late Harry Rudnick, says, "We have dealers, local people, and antique-shop owners, and they come from Pennsylvania, Maryland, Delaware, Virginia, D.C.—all over." The auction starts at 9:00 A.M. and continues to about 4:00 or 4:30 P.M. "We sell about eight hundred, nine hundred, a thousand items a day," says Rudnick.

Whenever there is a sale, the lunchroom is open for breakfast, lunch, and supper, and the menu changes every week. "Some days," adds Rudnick, "the women prepare spaghetti, fried chicken, or turkey, and there's hamburgers, hot dogs, and homemade soup." The price is about $5 for dinner.

Harry Rudnick and Sons is on Main Street, P.O. Box 190, Galena 21635. Call (301) 648–5601.

At the **Kent Museum** are indoor and outdoor exhibits of farm machinery from the last two centuries. The county gave a group of local farmers one hundred acres, twenty-five acres of which they ran on a volunteer basis to help defray the museum's operating costs. The museum was started about two decades ago, and people from the area and as far away as Pennsylvania have donated equipment to it.

Two early farm tractors mark the entrance, so you cannot miss it. Inside and outside the 40- by 150-foot building are exhibits on equipment used in planting and harvesting corn, wheat, soy, and other grains. You will see thrashers, tools from pre-industrial days, and modern-day combines and reapers. Other exhibits explain the work done by hand planters, automated corn planters, and tractors (the earliest tractor on display is a 1947 model).

Static displays can be tiresome, though, so on the last Saturday in July there is a thrashing demonstration, and on the first Saturday in August is a thrashing dinner. Of course, if you just happen by at other times of the year, when they are planting or otherwise tending to the fields, then you can watch them at work too. The museum also has a nature trail down to "Turner's Crick."

No admission is charged, but contributions are accepted. The Kent Museum is open 10:00 A.M. to 4:00 P.M. the first and third Saturday of the month from April through September, and it is located on Route 448 at Turner's Creek Public Landing, near Kennedyville. Call Aden Crouse (301–778–4928) or

Mary Lou Hurt (301–648–5142) for additional information.

Bicycle tours are popular in Kent County, and the chamber of commerce has prepared a booklet, The Kent County Bicycle Tour, for your information. Included are nine routes developed by the Baltimore Bicycling Club that range from 11 to 81 miles in length. As an example, the Pomona Warm-Up is "eleven miles of gently winding country roads with great views of the Chester River. A country store located at Pomona is a good eat or drink stop." The Pump House Primer is "eighty-one miles of gently rolling to flat riding through northern Kent County and on to Cecil County's historic Chesapeake and Delaware Canal Pump House Museum at Chesapeake City. Highlights are the Sassafras River, the museum, the C & D Canal, and Cecil County's beautiful horse farms." Note that you must walk your bike across the Sassafras River bridge.

In addition to tourism information, specific directions, and maps, a listing of restaurants, hotels, motels, campgrounds, and bed and breakfast establishments is available. Write to Patricia C. Piposzar, Executive Secretary, Kent County Chamber of Commerce, P.O. Box 146, 118 North Cross Street, Chestertown 21620, or call (301) 778–0416.

Queen Anne's County

The **Old Wye Grist Mill** is the oldest business in Queen Anne's County, in operation since 1671 or 1680, depending on whose reports you read. At least three mills have been located in this area for more than 300 years, giving the town of Wye Mills its name. Among its historic claims is the fact that ground cornmeal from this mill was purchased by Robert Morris, financier of the American Revolution, to be used as provisions for George Washington's army at Valley Forge in 1778.

Preservation Maryland, an organization to preserve the state's history and culture, has had the pleasure of working on this mill, which is particularly fascinating because as new equipment was developed, the old equipment was not hauled away and discarded. Therefore, there is a continuum of equipment to show the progress of milling over the years. They have completed work on the hydraulics, done most of the interior restoration, and soon will start a third phase to repair and restore a later roller mill and its exterior siding.

During your visit you can try your skill at Maryland's pre-industrial crafts, such as weaving, broom making, and hand milling. Also, depending on the season, you can buy corn-meal and a variety of flours—buckwheat, whole wheat, and sometimes rye.

A few of the volunteers dress in period costumes, but Barton McGuire, the master miller, does not. She is one of very few certified millers in the world, and she has been cer-tified for over twenty years. Maryland Preservation and the guests who visit the mill are fortunate to have her working here.

The Wye Mill is open Saturday and Sunday from 10:00 A.M. to 4:00 P.M. from March through December. It is open by appointment at other times. There is no admission charge, but they do ask for a donation. The mill is on Route 50, south of Route 662. The mailing address is P.O. Box 277, Wye Mills 21679, or you can contact the mill at (301) 827–6909 (a recording during the open season) or 685–2886.

Queen Anne's is known for its sprawling countryside and 900 farms, its terrific access to the Bay and Bay tributaries, and the genteel lifestyle it promotes. This country also has a reputation for some of the most horrendous traffic back-ups in recorded history! This happens when the drawbridge goes up over Kent Narrows as people are coming home on Sunday night from Ocean City. Happily, because of recent highway and bridge construction, memories are all that will remain of those 18-mile standing backups by the time you read this book.

Queen Anne's is becoming known for something else, too—factory outlet stores. One center, Eastern Shore Factory Stores, is at Piney Narrows Road, at the western end of the new bridge over Kent Narrows; the second is at Queenstown, just east of the Route 301-50 split (or merger depending on your direction).

The Eastern Shore outlet is the one we want to note, not because of the sensational bargains, but because of the **Farmer's Market,** operated here by several Amish families who travel from Lancaster, Pennsylvania, every Thursday, Friday, and Saturday. This is the place to stop for fresh-baked bread, meats, vegetables, and even some handicrafts and furniture. The market is at the Chesapeake Pottery, across the street from the Eastern Shore Factory Stores. Make sure you take time to stop by and sample the heritage of the Pennsylvania Dutch.

The market is open on Thursday and Friday from 10:00 A.M. to 6:00 P.M. and on Saturday from 9:00 A.M. to 3:00 P.M.

Another Amish market, where you can buy antiques, cotton candy, freshly fried potato chips, and shoofly pie is at the Crumpton Flea Market, every Wednesday from 3:00 to 9:00 P.M. If this location near Callister's Ferry (an old rope ferry operating between the north and south banks of the Chester River) looks familiar, it may be because the movie *Showboat* was filmed here.

You will notice a number of restaurants in Queen Anne's County, and a few rate some special mention: Hemingway's (Stevensville, 301–643–CRAB) and Poseidon (Routes 50 and 30 at Mears Point, 301–827–7605) both have excellent seafood and docking facilities.

The meeting place of the Eastern Shore since 1955, however, is **Holly's Restaurant**. It is noted for having the best milk shakes in the state. The tables are wooden and naked of frills like tablecloths; the waitresses are friendly, and the servings are enormous. You will find Holly's off Route 50 in Grasonville. Call (301) 827–8711.

Birdlife photographers and observers will welcome the new **Wildfowl Discovery Center** and the adjacent captive wildfowl collection in Grasonville. Surrounded by more than 300 acres of natural beauty, the center has a fascinating and colorful flock of wildfowl, including ducks, geese, and swans, and nearby are deer, red foxes, river otters, and bald eagles. Special screening allows you to quietly enter blinds so you can observe wildlife without disturbing it. The observation tower offers a panoramic view of the Chesapeake Bay and its wetlands.

The Wildfowl Trust of North America, founded in 1979, is responsible for the center, and you can be sure of programs, guided walks, workshops, a wetland festival, and lectures promoting stewardship of our dwindling wetland resources.

A gift shop and a shaded picnic area are also on site.

The Wildfowl Discovery Center is ½ mile from Route 18, off Perry Corner Road. Admission is $3 for adults, $2 for senior citizens and $1 for children. Dogs are not permitted. The center is open 9:00 A.M. to 5:00 P.M. Wednesday through Sunday. It is closed July 4, Thanksgiving, Christmas, and New Year's Day. For more information, write to Benedict J. Hren, Executive Director, The Wildfowl Trust of North America, P.O. Box 519, Grasonville 21638, or call (301) 827–6694.

For years the yellow and blue can of Old Bay Seasoning has been the only one to put on the table with that pile of steaming crabs. Then in the mid-1960s, cousins Joe Bernard and Mike Rossbach decided to can some Wye River Crab Soup, and that led to Wye River crab spices, Wye River potato chips, tortilla chips—these two young men have started an entire industry. Most of the ingredients for the white or red crab soup (claw meat, potatoes, tomatoes, lima beans, carrots, and green beans) are grown right here in Maryland. There is no factory to tour, for the soup is made in New Jersey and the chips are made in Ohio, but you can stop by the headquarters and buy from their full line of products.

Wye River Products is in Queenstown at Green Spring Road, Route 50. Call (301) 643–2666.

Almost as good as a platter of crabs are the biscuits from **Orrell House and Bakery**. Hundreds of dozens of these heavy biscuits, which started as a source of pin money for Mrs. Orrell about fifty years ago, go out to local stores and shops around the country. The recipe, which is flour, water, salt, lard, sugar, and baking powder, originated in Southern Maryland and the Eastern Shore during plantation days. It produces a biscuit that is soft and doughy on the inside and hard on the outside. There are some who say these biscuits are not any good until they feel like hockey pucks, and many swear by them as teething biscuits. Believe us, just because they feel hard does not mean they have gone stale. A special pick is used to prick the tops of the biscuits (in an "O" and cross design) so they will not blister and burn.

The bakery is open on Wednesday from 7:00 A.M. to 2:00 P.M., Thursday from 2:00 to 11:00 P.M., and Friday from 7:00 A.M. to 12:00 noon. The address is Orrell House and Bakery, P.O. Box 7, Wye Mills 21679. Turn right at the stoplight at

Chesapeake College and drive to the famous Wye Oak Tree. Orrell House is between the oak and Wye parish. Call (301) 822–2065.

For more tourism information, write to Tina Miles, Tourism, Queen Anne's County Tourism, County Office Building, Centreville 21617, or call (301) 758–2300.

Talbot County

Tourists coming through this area—about 100,000 of you each year going to St. Michaels—stop to see the Chesapeake Bay Maritime Museum, the Customs House, the Robert Morris Inn, and Tilghman Island (with a meal at Harrison's Chesapeake House).

The Chesapeake Bay Maritime Museum receives by far the most tourists, and well it should. But there are two small, privately owned museums, that may also be worth your time.

Millie Curtis' **Museum of Costume** in St. Michaels contains some unique displays. On exhibit are gowns worn by former presidents' wives, pantaloons worn by Mrs. Abraham Lincoln, and a vest worn by Clark Gable in *Gone With the Wind*. Rooms are filled with ornate nineteenth- and early twentieth-century gowns. Curtis has been accumulating her collection since 1940. She has been known to greet guests wearing one of her costumes.

The white frame house was erected by shipbuilder and sea captain Lewis Tarr in 1843. It is restored so you can see the original pine floors, the board-and-batten doors, and other aspects of the architecture.

The Museum of Costume is open daily from 11:00 A.M. to 5:00 P.M., April through November. The suggested donation is $2. Children under ten are admitted free. The address is 400 St. Mary's Square, St. Michaels 21663. Call (301) 745–5154.

St. Mary's Square Museum exhibits items of significance to the local history and culture, not just of St. Michaels, but of the land between Tilghman and Royal Oak, called the Bay 100—that portion of land which could be defended by one hundred armed men. Two buildings are used for this museum, one of them dating to 1820 and one to 1860, the latter referred to as the "Teetotum" building because it looks like the shape of a child's four-sided top of that name.

In the 1820 building are artifacts from 1800 to 1850; in the kitchen area are items from 1850 to 1900; and in the Teetotum room are articles from colonial days to about 1950. Curator Horace Wilson says most of these buildings were moved from other sites in the area. This museum was opened in 1964 by a group of local citizens, and although it sits on the original St. Mary's Square and is on city property, the museum is entirely self-supported. A group of twenty board members runs the operation.

It is open from May through October on Saturday, Sunday, and on holidays from 10:00 A.M. to 4:00 P.M. or by appointment. There is no admission charge, but donations are accepted. For additional information, call (301) 745–9561 or talk with Horace Wilson at (301) 745–9057.

Laura Ashley fans rejoice. Sir Bernard Ashley (who with his late wife Laura founded the clothing and furnishings empire) has purchased the **Inn at Perry Cabin** in St. Michaels. This inn is the first of what is expected to be a number of Ashley Inns along the East Coast. The inn has been expanded from six to nineteen rooms, and the kitchen has been modernized. The menu features traditional Chesapeake recipes with an emphasis on local products. The towels, sheets, wallpaper, and other decorative items are all from the Laura Ashley line.

The Inn at Perry Cabin is at 308 Watkins Lane, St. Michaels 21663. The phone number is (301) 745–5178.

At the Easton plant of the **Black & Decker** tool company, they make consumer appliances, such as blenders, vacuum cleaners, mixers, and hedge trimmers, as well as professional equipment, such as screw drivers, cordless drills, jig saws, and small angle grinders. You can take a thirty-five-minute tour of the process, wearing safety goggles, in the daytime or the evening, because the plant operates three shifts around the clock. You will see the entire process, from creating the parts to assembling the final tools. Most of the consumer goods are done by hand work, not by robots; but the professional tools are primarily produced by robots.

They prefer groups not larger than twelve people, but can handle groups in multiples of twelve by calling in more volunteers to conduct the tour. They do not allow anyone under sixteen. They like at least three days' notice. The plant is at 515 Glebe Road, Easton 21601. For additional information, call David Steibel at (301) 820–2533.

Bed and breakfast establishments seem to belong in large Victorian homes, and the **John S. McDaniel House Bed and Breakfast**, operated by Bill and Genie Kramedas, fits that description to a "t." Built around 1890, the house has a high octagonal tower (a great sitting room), a hip-roof with dormers, and a porch that runs across the front and part of the south side of the house. Each of the seven guest rooms is spacious and bright and equipped with air conditioning and a ceiling fan. Fortunately, the house is located within walking distance of historic Easton.

The John S. McDaniel House is a member of the Inns of the Eastern Shore, a choice selection of bed and breakfast establishments located on the eastern shore of Maryland and Virginia. Room rates run from $50 to $60 (add $5 for Friday and Saturday from May through Thanksgiving) with a continental breakfast served between 8:00 and 10:00 A.M.

The John S. McDaniel House Bed and Breakfast is located at 14 North Aurora Street, Easton 21601. Call (301) 822–3704 for information and reservations.

One of the ten remaining ferries in service in Maryland is the **Tred Avon Ferry,** which crosses the Tred Avon River and connects Oxford to Belleview. It has been operating since 1683, and is said to be the oldest "free-running" (not cable-connected), privately owned ferry in the country. It operates all year with a capacity of ten cars and fifteen passengers. The crossing takes seven minutes and costs $4.00 per car and driver and $.25 for each additional person. Bikes are $1.50, and motorcycles are $2.00 each. This is a particularly photogenic ferry crossing at sunset, as the boats are all at their Oxford harbor moorings, with their masts standing out against the skyline. Next to the Oxford landing is the custom house, a replica of the original built in pre-revolutionary days when Oxford was an official port of entry.

To reach the Tred Avon Ferry from Easton, take Route 33 and Route 333; from Bellevue take Route 33 and Route 329 to Royal Oak and follow the signs. Call (301) 226–5408 for further information.

Wye Oak State Park is considered a "big little" place: The park in total size is only twenty-nine acres, but it contains the 450-year-old Maryland state tree, the Wye Oak. This tree measures a huge 37 feet in circumference and is considered to be the largest and finest of its species in the United States.

The state bought the tree and one acre around it in 1939—the first time any state ever purchased one tree just to preserve it. Over time, more land was added to make this a state park. It was the first state park to be fully accessible to the handicapped, perhaps because it's so small that accessibility was easy to create. Wye Oak State Park is south of Wye Mills on Route 662.

You have heard that big oaks come from little acorns, and, of course, the opposite is true—little acorns come from big oaks. The Maryland Forest, Park and Wildlife Service gathers the acorns, plants them, and lets them grow for a couple of years until they are established seedlings. You can purchase a Wye Oak seedling from the state for about $6 plus tax if you live in Maryland. They are shipped in March in time for the spring planting. They can not be shipped to Arizona, California, Florida, Louisiana, or Oregon due to quarantine restrictions.

These are the cutest little trees, no bigger in diameter than your little finger, but they produce mature-size leaves, about six or seven of them the first year. They do not grow as rapidly as, say, a maple tree, but they are of substantial size within a decade. And, who knows, 400 years from now there may be a champion tree in your yard.

To order Wye Oak seedlings, write to the Nursery Manager, Buckingham Forest Tree Nursery, Harmans 21077. You must give a full street address; a post office box number is inadequate for delivery.

For more tourism information write to Kathy Magruder, Talbot County Chamber of Commerce, P.O. Box 1366, 7 Federal Street, Easton 21601, or call (301) 822–4606.

Off the Beaten Path on the Southern Eastern Shore

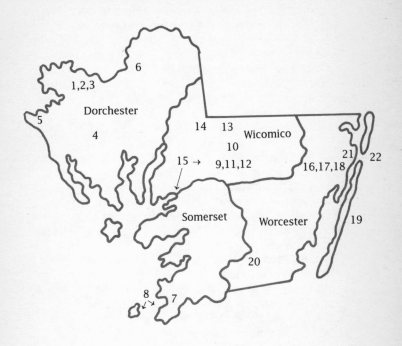

1. Dorchester County Public Library
2. Dorchester Arts Center
3. Wild Goose Amber Beer
4. Blackwater National Wildlife Refuge
5. Taylor's Island General Store
6. East New Market
7. Captain's Galley Restaurant
8. Ferryboats
9. Hall of Fame Tennis Classic
10. Salisbury Pewter
11. Chesapeake Shipbuilding
12. Wildfowl Art Museum
13. High Ball
14. Mason-Dixon Line
15. Ferryboats
16. Berlin walking tour
17. Taylor House Museum
18. Atlantic Hotel
19. Assateague Island National Seashore
20. Pocomoke City Post Office
21. Airplane advertising
22. Phillips Crab House

Southern Eastern Shore

We have reached the eastern-most portion of Maryland, the southern part of the Delmarva Peninsula (*DEL*aware, *MAR*yland, and *V*irgini*A*), where James Michener did the research for his popular novel *Chesapeake.* This is where you see as well as hear about those unfamiliar boats, the skipjack, the bugeye, and the bungy.

You also will see "June bugs," the thousands of kids who invade the ocean beaches and boardwalks every summer to work at jobs and tanning.

Explore and enjoy the dissimilarities you will find within a few short miles. Stop by a library to see a mural painted by an artist who is so popular these days that the library could not afford another mural like it. Find budding artists at the Dorchester Arts Center. Try a new beer, search for bald eagles and great blue herons, mingle with area residents at the general store, and see centuries-old homes that have not needed restoration because they have been so well maintained over the years.

Ride the ferryboats, eat at some of the best seafood restaurants in the country, examine the fine local examples of duck-decoy carving, and take a peek at some of the prettiest passenger boats and ferryboats being built these days. Take time to locate the Mason-Dixon line; it surprises most people that the line not only separates Pennsylvania and Maryland, but also delineates the Delaware–Maryland border.

Last, but not least, get some sand between your toes and contemplate the treasures of America in Miniature.

Dorchester County

Years before we thought about writing this book, we stopped at the **Dorchester County Public Library** and admired a wonderful mural of Eastern Shore scenes being painted by prominent Chesapeake Bay artist John Moll. That creation stayed in our mental and metal filing drawers all these years.

Moll became familiar to James Michener when the author was researching *Chesapeake*, and they collaborated on a subsequent book because Michener thought the Oxford resident "not only captured the flavor of my subject but had earned the enthusiasm of those who love the Chesapeake."

Moll's lithographs are known for their faithful characterization of the skipjacks and Bay lighthouses he loves. His Christmas cards with Oxford and Annapolis scenes or Baycraft portraits are still popular, and John Moll oils hang in the permanent collection of the Eastern Academy of Arts and in the historic Robert Morris Inn in Oxford. Bob Porter of the Framing Place, 125 Kemp Lane in Easton (301–820–7272), has the largest collection of Moll's work and still handles his notepaper, place mats, and reproductions of his sketches done as mounted prints. The Historical Society of Easton did a four-month retrospective of Moll's work in 1989.

This gives you an idea how popular an artist is represented in the Dorchester County Public Library. The address of the library is 303 Gay Street, Cambridge 21613 (301–228–7331).

The **Dorchester Arts Center** was founded in 1970 and has between 400 and 500 members (mostly from the Cambridge area) including potters, photographers, quilters, stained-glass artists, and basket makers. In addition to regular classes in these and other crafts, the center has two galleries where local work is exhibited and sold. Each month a new exhibit opens with a reception.

During the year, the center sponsors a variety of music, dance, and educational programs, a number of which are free to the public. Each September the sidewalks along the historic, brick High Street, with its beautiful period homes, are festooned with the best work of eighty of Dorchester County artists and crafters. A poster of the Frederic C. Malkus Bridge by Church Prahl, Jr., (dated April 25, 1987, the opening day of the new bridge) is available for $10 and benefits the arts center. The center is located at 120 High Street, Cambridge 21613; call (301) 228–7782 for more information.

John Neal Mullican is another artist represented in Cambridge. He did the great blue heron statue at the intersection of High and Water streets, and his work also appears in Upper Marlboro (Prince George's County) by the County Administration Building; at the new Washington Suburban Sanitary Commission headquarters building (Montgomery and Prince George's counties); and in the State House in Annapolis (Anne Arundel County). Mullican is nearly a native Marylander (he was born in Washington, D.C., but moved to Maryland within a few years), and although he has had some lessons, he is basically a self-taught artist. The Cambridge statue was commissioned to promote and commemorate the establishment of the Blackwater Wildlife Refuge, south of town.

From the visual art we move to the art of brewing, which brings us to the new Cambridge microbrewery. The first batch of **Wild Goose Amber Beer**, billed as "The Only Beer for Crabs," was produced in early November of 1989. According to brewmaster Alan Pugsley, Wild Goose tastes like a pale English ale. "Chesapeake's Own" microbrewery license allows them to have a bar or restaurant for on-site ales; however, at this time they are only distributing the beer off site. Tours of the brewery are available through the old Phillips Packing House, which was, during World War II, the second-largest soup-packing house in the country (Campbell's was first). The tour lasts about an hour, and naturally it includes a wee little taste. Individuals can tour for free; groups are about $2.50 per person. Wild Goose Amber Beer microbrewery is at 20 Washington Street, Cambridge 21613. Call (301) 221–1121.

As mentioned, the **Blackwater National Wildlife Refuge** is south of Cambridge. We have spent many hours here trying to photograph the great blue heron. The refuge is a marvelous sanctuary with a tower for climbing (about fifty or sixty steps) for an overall view of the area. There used to be an admission charge, but since bald eagles began to nest along one of the main roads, prohibiting traffic, the park has stopped charging admission.

The U.S. Fish and Wildlife Service has agreed to purchase an additional 774 acres for $468,000, which brings the total acreage to 16,698. Besides the bald eagle and the great blue heron, you will see black ducks, the endangered Delmarva fox squirrel, and countless other animals and birds. Do stop by in November and December when the Canada geese fly over. Take your insect repellent in July and August, if you must go then at all.

Great Blue Heron Statue

Drive south on Route 16 to Route 335 in Church Creek, to Key Wallace Drive and the signs. Blackwater National Wildlife Refuge is open Monday through Friday from 8:00 A.M. to 4:00 P.M. and on weekends from 9:00 A.M. to 5:00 P.M., Labor Day through Memorial Day. Call (301) 228–2677 for further information.

The food is good where the locals gather, and one of these gathering places is on Taylor's Island at the **Taylor's Island General Store**, just across Slaughter Creek Bridge, southwest of Cambridge. The best sandwiches and soups in the area are served here, and you will not go wrong with Erlyne Twining's crab soup, oyster chowder, chili, or lima bean soup; meat-based soups sell for $2.00 and non-meat soups sell for $1.50. The crab cakes contain a quarter-pound of crab meat each and go for $3.00. Quite a bargain. Erlyne, her husband Perry, and their son Terry also sell ice, beer, soda, gas, and groceries and have an interesting display of "old-time stuff" from former general stores.

You will find signs that spell it Taylors Island—usually state signs—and people who spell it Taylor's—usually the locals, because they say the land originally was called Taylor's Folly after the Mr. Taylor who bought the land. We side with the locals on this one. Taylor's Island General Store is on Route 16, Taylor's Island (301–397–3733).

A number of towns in Maryland are architecturally historic, and the buildings have not needed much outside restoration. **East New Market**, originally Crossroads, is one of those towns. At each of the four entrances to the town stands a church. On Route 16 South, it is the Trinity United Methodist; Route 16 North, St. Stephen's Episcopal; Route 14 West, First Baptist; and Route 14 East, Salem German Evangelical and Reformed Church. These churches reflect the diverse denominations represented in this area.

Indians dwelled here; the first European mention of the region was in a grant to Henry Sewell dated 1659 in London, England. The first white settler is believed to have been a Quaker, John Edmondson, who came from Virginia in the 1660s to seek religious freedom. Edmondson was followed by the O'Sullivane family; and this historic district contains almost all of their early residences. These homes are the core of the town's colonial architecture, but among the almost seventy-five buildings there are a number from the eighteenth, nineteenth, and twentieth centuries. Many of the brick walks laid in 1884 still exist.

The East New Market Heritage Foundation sponsors an annual Candlelight Tour in late December, with admission set at $7 for adults and $6 for Foundation members and seniors. Children twelve years and under, accompanied by an adult, are free.

The East New Market Heritage Foundation is at P.O. Box 112, East New Market 21631. Call (301) 943–8713.

For additional tourism information, write to Chuck Adkinson, Director, Dorchester County Tourism, P.O. Box 307, Cambridge 21613, or call (301) 228–3234.

Somerset County

Every endeavor from the sublime to the ridiculous is represented at two Somerset County museums, both well documented in most state tourism brochures. Depending on your available time, you will want to stop by the Eastern Shore Early Americana Museum at Route 667 and Old Westover Road, in Hudsons Corner. Pack rats and Americana lovers have Lawrence W. Burgess to thank for being a certifiable scavenger. This museum, housed in a converted poultry house, is a monument to accumulating. It contains a little bit of everything, from political buttons to oyster-tonging forks. For hours and information call (301) 623–8324. On the other hand, there is the Governor J. Millard Tawes Historical Museum in Crisfield, with its exhibits pertaining to the late governor, the history and development of the Crisfield seafood industry, local art and folklore, and the life of the area from Indian times to the present. Call (301) 968–2501 for further information. These two museums may contain items about the same time, place, and people, but they sure do come out different.

With a little time, you also might want to stop by the Teackle Mansion on Sunday afternoon or visit the hundred-room EconoLodge in Princess Anne, which is the first fully operational franchised hotel operated and managed by student interns; they participate in the Hotel and Restaurant

Management program at University of Maryland Eastern Shore.

You might want to try some seafood, for this is the self-proclaimed "Seafood Capital of the World"; or take a ferry out to Smith Island. For both of these pleasures, you could not come to a more perfect place.

As you drive down to the end of Main Street to watch the boating activity, stop for a meal at the **Captain's Galley Restaurant**. They are not immodest when they claim to be the "home of the world's best crab cake." The crabmeat is caught and picked fresh daily from the Chesapeake waters and then lightly seasoned with herbs and spices. For a real treat, try the 100 percent backfin crabmeat, fried or broiled. Owner Rich Tonelli's soft-shell–crab sandwich is no slouch either, and during cold-weather days, there is nothing better than one of their apple dumplings to warm up the insides. The local artwork is also a special treat.

Captain's Galley is at the end of Main Street, well within sight of the relatively new pavilion at the end of the city wharf. It overlooks the beautiful Tangier Sound. As you dine on delectable seafood, you can watch the watermen of the Chesapeake bring in the bounty of its waters. Call (301) 968–1636 for information or reservations.

Four **ferryboats** operate out of Crisfield; there are three to Smith Island (in Maryland) and one to Tangier Island (in Virginia). At Smith Island, the only inhabited island accessible exclusively by boat in Maryland, you will see crabs shedding their shells, the village of Rhodes Point, crab shanties, and the workboats at Tylerton.

The *Captain Tyler II* travels to Smith Island daily from Memorial Day to September 30. This 65-foot, riverboat-style paddlewheeler was built in New York during World War II and was used as a cargo vessel for the military. The departure time for the one-hour-and-ten-minute crossing is 12:30 P.M. and the boat leaves Smith Island at 5:30 P.M. It takes up to 150 passengers and bicycles are permitted. The fare is $15.00 for an adult and $7.50 for children (6 to 12) and includes free bus transportation to Rhodes Point. Contact Tyler's Cruises, Rhodes Point 21858 (301–425–2771).

The *Captain Jason* is a smaller but faster boat that takes only fifty passengers (and bikes) for a $10 round trip, and it operates all year. It departs Crisfield at 12:30 P.M. and 5:00

P.M. for overnight stays at Smith Island, and it returns at 8:00 A.M. and 4:00 P.M. The mailing address is P.O. Box 205, Tylerton 21866; call (301) 425–4471.

The *Island Bell II* is the only mail boat operating in Maryland; it has a capacity of fifty passengers, assuming there is not too much mail. The one-hour crossing leaves Crisfield at 12:30 P.M. and 5:00 P.M. and returns from Smith Island at 8:00 A.M. and 4:30 P.M. The fare is $5 per person, but there is a $2 charge for bicycles. The address is P.O. Box 12, Ewell 21824, or call (301) 425–4271 or –2201.

The *Steven Thomas* is a 90-foot cruise boat that handles 300 or more passengers on its one-hour-and-fifteen-minute crossing to Tangier Island from Crisfield. It operates daily from Memorial Day through October, and group reservations are strongly suggested. The fare is $14 per person round trip and bicycles are permitted at $3 per bike. Departure times are set at 12:30 P.M. with a return at 5:15 P.M. Write to the *Steven Thomas*, Crisfield 21817, or call (301) 968–2338.

The *Captain Evans* ferry operates between Smith Island and Reedville, Virginia between May and mid-October, departing Reedville at 10:00 A.M. and 4:00 P.M. The 150-passenger boat costs $16 per person, $8 for children, and $2 for bikes.

One other ferry, the *Captain Tyler*, runs between Point Lookout State Park and Smith Island (see St. Mary's County).

Two of Maryland's ten ferries—the Whitehaven and Upper ferries—operate between Somerset and Wicomico counties. Check the Wicomico County section for additional details.

For further tourism information, write to Sandie Marriner, Director, Somerset County Tourism, P.O. Box 243, Princess Anne 21853. Call (301) 651–2968 or (800) 521–9189 (nationwide).

Wicomico County

For a while Salisbury was becoming known as the Tennis Capital of the World—well, at least in some circles. Names like Bill Riordan, Jimmy Connors, and Harry Hopman were easily bandied about like so many tennis balls in a pregame volley. Tennis pros came to this town (Riordan did have a dress shop here); it became the smallest town on the international tennis circuit. Instead of staying in hotels, players stayed in the homes of local residents. Then a fire came, and tennis went.

Now, however, tennis is coming back with the Rotary Eastern Shore **Hall of Fame Tennis Classic** in March. In 1990 Vijay Amritraj, the Russian Alex Metreveli, Stan Smith, and Ilie Nastase were four of the eight grand old masters of tennis who agreed to participate in the "tennis legends" event. The plans are good for the event to continue to come to Salisbury. Of course, the players now stay in a hotel, but residents still love tennis, and there are dozens of tennis courts around town. For more information about the Tennis Classic, contact Lee Whaley at the Wicomico Youth and Civic Center, Glen Avenue Extended, Salisbury 21801 (301–543–4414).

Salisbury Pewter, although only formed in 1980, is a company of dedicated crafters who believe that although modern technology can be helpful, the most important part of their business is to maintain the heritage of their craft. Many of their methods have been handed down for centuries and each piece of pewter is meticulously handcrafted. Their pewter ware contains no lead. They offer a customizing service, and there is one wall with letters of appreciation from highly elected officials for a series of pewter pieces created for an appreciation award.

On weekdays you can see the crafters at work, going from raw product to a finished piece of art. Salisbury Pewter is on Highway 13 North. Their mailing address is P.O. Box 2475, Salisbury 21801; call (301) 546–1188 or (800) 824–4700 (out of state).

So you are driving down near Fitzwater Street or along the Wicomico River, and you see this 200-foot yacht under construction or going down the waterway. No, you are not imagining things.

Salisbury is the home of the **Chesapeake Shipbuilding** company. There are shipbuilders and naval architects and the most successful and experienced "passenger boat" shipyard in the United States. They make catamaran cruise ships, riverboat cruise ships, dinner restaurant vessels, car and truck ferries, and passenger excursion ferries, which operate along the entire Eastern Seaboard, the Great Lakes, the Mississippi River, the Pacific Northwest, Canada, and Panama. The restaurant boat you cruised on last week or last year may well have been built here. Their coastal cruise ships are the largest in the nation that meet U.S. Coast Guard "Subchapter T" regulations. The late, lamented American Cruise Line ships, which used to cruise the intracoastal waterway, came from this shipyard.

Chesapeake Shipbuilding is at 710 Fitzwater Street, Salisbury 21801. Call (301) 742–4900 for more information.

The **Wildfowl Art Museum** of the Ward Foundation in Holloway Hall at Salisbury State College houses what is perhaps the largest collection of decorative bird carvings in the world, including many antique decoys. The Foundation is named for internationally renowned waterfowl carvers and painters Lem and Steve Ward of Crisfield, Maryland. During their lifetimes, they produced more than 25,000 decoys and decorative birds, which the men called "counterfeits." Their workshop has been recreated, and on display are more than one hundred fine examples of their old classic hunting decoys as well as their decoratives. Lem did most of the painting, while Steve did most of the carving. Steve died in 1976, and Lem died in 1984 at the age of eighty-eight. The collection is fascinating and valuable, and soon it will have a new home, built just for the collection.

A gift shop on site has a wide selection of wildfowl-related items. Hours are Tuesday through Saturday from 10:00 A.M. to 5:00 P.M. and from 1:00 to 5:00 P.M. on Sunday. Guided group tours are available. Admission is $1 for adults; there is no charge to children under twelve, senior citizens, and Salisbury State College students. The museum is in Holloway Hall at Salisbury State College, at Camden and College avenues. For further information contact the Ward Foundation at 655 South Salisbury Boulevard, Salisbury 21801, or call them at (301) 742–4988.

The Ward Foundation was established to save the art form of decoy carving, which has grown from the carving of working decoys designed to catch a bird to decorative carving of collector's items. The Foundation's annual summer seminar at Salisbury State College offers hands-on instruction by some of the most talented artists and teachers in the field, such as Ernie Muehlmatt, Pat Godin, Bill Koelpin, Bob Guge, Larry Bath, and Jim Sprankle. Intensive, week-long sessions cover such topics as anatomy and research, shaping, texturing, burning, priming and painting, and various brush techniques. Room and board are provided on campus. For information about the seminars, contact the Ward Foundation at the address given above.

If you have heard the railroad expression about "high balling it down the road" and wondered what it means, take a visit to Delmar to see the **High Ball.** (Delmar is a combination of two states, Delaware and Maryland; in town, State Street straddles the border. There was a time when the two halves—two mayors, two town councils, two school systems—fought over municipal functions, but things have been patched up for some time.) Along the tracks near State Street you will see a large white ball, which was raised on high to signify that the line was clear, giving rise to the term "high balling." A small museum is housed in the caboose next to the tracks, and it is open by appointment by calling George Truitt (302–846–2654).

Driving along the flat stretch of Route 54 west of Delmar near Mardela Springs, you will parallel the southern end of the east-west section of the **Mason-Dixon line.** One could even say this is the cornerstone of the Mason-Dixon line. A double crownstone was installed in 1768 by Charles Mason and Jeremiah Dixon to settle the boundary disputes between the Penn and Calvert families, whose coats of arms it bears. There is a small parking lot and a brick and wrought-iron pavilion protecting the stones.

Called the Middle Point monument because it marks the middle of the Delmarva Peninsula, it also is a triangulation point of the National Geodetic Survey. The stone was broken off by vandals at ground level in 1983, and another stone originally set by colonial surveyors in 1760 was defaced by removal of the Calvert coat of arms. The Maryland Department of Natural Resources and Delaware's State Boundary Commission jointly replaced the monument on October 24, 1985. Protective grill work to completely enclose the pavilion was also replaced. The previous grill work was erected by the Daughters of the American Revolution.

Skipjacks can be seen in the watermen's villages of Deal Island, Chance, and Wenona. Over Labor Day weekend this last fleet of working sailboats race in the Tangier Sound of Deal Island in the annual Skipjack Races.

Two **ferryboats** continue service, survivors of the many that once linked water-isolated communities on the Wicomico River, between Wicomico and Somerset counties. Both are small, both are free, and they operate all year, weather conditions and tides permitting.

The Upper Ferry crosses between Allen and Route 349, and takes about three minutes. It is run year-round during daylight hours with on-demand service, except on Sunday and major holidays. The Upper Ferry is an outboard-motor–propelled cable ferryboat with no name. A ferry has been running here since at least 1897; the current one has a capacity of two cars plus six passengers, with a maximum vehicle size of five tons gross weight. Bicycles are permitted.

The Whitehaven–Mt. Vernon Cable Ferry, called the Whitehaven Ferry, is 6 miles downriver from the Upper Ferry, and connects Whitehaven to Widgeon; it has been operating since 1690. The modern ferryboat, the *Som-Wico*, takes about five minutes for a crossing and can hold three cars plus ten passengers. Bikes are permitted. Whitehaven is the oldest incorporated town on the river and once was a vital deepwater port and shipbuilding area.

Both ferries are run by the Wicomico County Road Department. Call (301) 548–4872 for more information.

Contact Lewis R. Carman, Tourism Director, or Millie Seward, Assistant at the Convention and Visitor Bureau, Wicomico Youth and Civic Center, Glen Avenue Extended, Salisbury 21801, for further details on tourism, or you can call (301) 548–4914 or 749–8687 (twenty-four—hour information recording).

Worcester County

The town of Berlin in Worcester (pronounced like "rooster") County has no connection to the city in Germany; instead, it is a corruption of Burley Inn, the name of the site on which it was constructed.

A guided map for a **Berlin walking tour** includes a town park and monument dedicated to Commodore Stephen Decatur, a native of Berlin. The oldest homes were built in the Federal period; later homes adopted the Victorian style, and twentieth-century homes are typified by the "bungalow." Also on the guided map, which can be picked up at local businesses, are a local business directory and a calendar of events.

A typical Federal-style post-and-beam house is the **Taylor House Museum**. It was built about 1825 and now is used as the town museum. The gable-front house features a Palladian window with Victorian glass, restored wood graining, and a magnificent front doorway with butterfly modillions, sunbursts, and fluted, engaged columns. The house was supposed to be destroyed and replaced by a new post office and parking lot, but it was saved in 1981 by the Berlin Heritage Foundation. With $100,000 in private donations from the community, the house was restored from its dilapidated condition.

Although Robert J. Henry, who was instrumental in bringing the railroad to Berlin, lived in the house, the most famous occupant was Calvin B. Taylor, the founder of the Calvin B. Taylor Banking Company, which is still in existence. Much of the house and appointments are original to the times that various occupants lived in the house, including C. B. Taylor's bank desk with its hidden doors on the side and front.

Taylor House is at 208 North Main Street at the intersection with Baker Street, across from the Stevenson Methodist Church in Berlin. The house is open Monday, Wednesday, Friday, and Sunday from 1:00 to 4:00 P.M. and for special events, such as concerts. Call (301) 641–1019. There is no admission charge.

In the middle of the historic district is the **Atlantic Hotel,** a faithfully restored 1895 Victorian hostelry which was rescued from the depths of distress to become this showpiece, named to the National Register of Historic Places in 1980.

Each of the sixteen guest rooms (each with private bath) is beautifully furnished with antiques and is unique in its decor. We understand Paige Hammond, wife of Edward Hammond, local attorney and one of the partners in the Atlantic Hotel project, was responsible for selecting the antiques and color schemes. Rich green and burgundy, delicate rose and aqua, deep mahogany tones, tassels, braid, lace, and crochet help transport you to a gentler time and

136

Atlantic Hotel

quieter pace. A parlor—for reading, letter writing, or conversation—is on the second floor. If you must have television in your room, the hotel staff is quite willing to provide one for you.

Continental breakfast is provided. The dinner menu changes periodically to reflect seasonal availabilities, but you might find lobster sauté stuffed scallops, sole paupiettes, a seafood sampler, or selections "from the land." One interesting offering, either as an appetizer or as part of the sampler, is their coconut shrimp, which is jumbo shrimp dredged in coconut, pan-fried golden brown, and finished with a sweet pepper and mango chutney. Stephen Jacques is general manager and chef, and you should not be surprised if he comes to your table to personally tell you what is on the menu for the day.

The Atlantic Hotel Inn and Restaurant is located at 2 North Main Street, Berlin 21811. Call (301) 641–3589 for information or reservations.

Seven miles east of Berlin is **Assateague Island National Seashore**, which is reached by Route 611. Nearly 150,000 people visit this seashore annually. A two-room visitor center is open for interpretive classes and exhibits, which include a small "touch tank" of marine life. During a visit here you can take a guided walk; view a demonstration on how to catch blue crabs, clams, and ribbed mussels (mighty tasty steamed or sautéed in butter); or you might join a naturalist at the Old Ferry Landing to explore the ¾-mile width of Assateague Island. You will travel by foot and bike or car from the salt marsh to the pounding surf, discovering relationships between the various barrier island life zones.

The famed Chincoteague ponies can be seen on Assateague, for two herds of the wild ponies make their home here. The herds are separated by a fence at the Maryland-Virginia state line. Managed by the National Park Service on the Maryland side, horses are often seen around roads and campgrounds. The horses sold at auction every July are on the Virginia side. No road connects the two states within the park.

Supposedly, the horses are descended from domesticated stock that grazed on the island as early as the seventeenth century; Eastern Shore planters put them here to avoid mainland taxes and fencing requirements. Smaller than horses, these shaggy, sturdy ponies are well adapted to their harsh seashore environment. Marsh and dune grasses supply the bulk of their food, and they obtain water from freshwater impoundments or natural ponds.

Although they appear tame, they are unpredictable and can inflict serious wounds by kicking and biting. The Park Service strongly recommends that you do not pet or feed the ponies.

You may find great blue herons, snowy egrets, dungins, American widgeons, black-crowned night herons, Peregrine falcons, and numerous other birds on the Maryland side, but they are more easily seen on the Virginia side.

Legend has it that Edward Teach (Blackbeard the Pirate) kept one of his fourteen wives, a base of operations, and buried treasure on Assateague. The visitor center is open daily from 8:30 A.M. to 5:00 P.M. For more information, call (301) 641–2120.

The VIEWTRAIL 100 signs you will see on secondary state and county roads mark a scenic bicycle trail, which is maintained by the Worcester 4-H Older Youth. You can join the trail in Berlin as it sweeps down to Pocomoke City, past the access to Furnace Town, Nassawango Creek Cypress Swamp, Milburn Landing on the north bank of the Pocomoke River, Mt. Zion One-Room School Museum, and many other interesting attractions. The Pocomoke River is the northernmost swamp river on the East Coast, and along its banks are cypress trees (used to make our country's first ships) and Spanish moss. Here you can see eagles, egrets, hawks, and vultures as well.

Another bike trail, the Beach to Bay Indian Trail, goes from Crisfield on the Chesapeake Bay in Somerset County up to Princess Anne, Snow Hill, Berlin, and Ocean City. It was opened in the spring of 1988, and it is jointly sponsored by Somerset and Worcester Tourism, Ocean City, the State of Maryland, and the departments of Economic and Employment Development, Transportation, Natural Resources, and Housing and Community Development. For more Maryland bike trail information, call (301) 333–1663. For travel information about Ocean City, call (800) 49–BEACH (in Maryland) or (800) 62–OCEAN in Delaware, Pennsylvania, Virginia, West

Virginia, New Jersey, southeast New York, and Washington, D.C.

A carved-wood relief sculpture in polychrome, called The Power of Communication, hangs over the postmaster's door in the **Pocomoke City Post Office**. Perna Krick of Baltimore executed the commission in 1940. The figure of an Indian with an airplane reflects the history of the area, from Indian tradition to the development of communication, from primitive methods to present-day service.

Ms. Krick was born in Ohio in 1909, and attended the Dayton Art Institute. She studied under J. Maxwell Miller at the Rinehard School of Sculpture in Baltimore, receiving two European traveling scholarships. By the time she received this commission from the Federal Works Agency, she had exhibited at the Baltimore Art Museum, the Pennsylvania Academy of Fine Arts, and the Architectural League in New York.

One of the traditional sights around Ocean City is the airplanes flying banners about 200 feet above sea level. Robert Bunting of Berlin bought a small crop duster in 1982 and started **airplane advertising** by flying up and down the beach with banner messages. The business is so popular that a half-dozen fabric-covered, single-engine aircraft are used for this kind of advertising.

Each banner has forty or fewer letters and may carry a marriage proposal or tell you about the newest restaurant in town. If you would like to have them carry your message for the world to see while they "fly low and slow," it will cost between $50 and $160 per banner. If you go watch the ground crew rig the planes, you will see them set the banner between two upright poles that are 6 feet apart. (It is said that if the ground crew is feeling prankish, they will set the poles only 2 feet apart.) Then the plane flies about eighty-five miles per hour to pick up the banner. Usually the pilot makes it on the first trip, but it sometimes has taken as many as six tries to hook a banner. You are looking at some first-class flying.

Between Memorial Day and Labor Day, each pilot will log about 500 hours flying from 10:00 A.M. to 4:00 P.M., seven days a week, and together they will fly as many as 110 banners in one day, although the average is about forty-five to fifty.

Ocean City is a family-oriented party town on the ocean. It is 7 miles north of Berlin. Thousands of college kids ("June bugs") come here every summer to work and vacation. There is plenty to do, from kite flying (probably our favorite activity), to boating, to fishing, to checking to make sure the draft beer is kept at the right temperature.

As with any resort, there are dozens (if not hundreds) of restaurants, eateries, bars, and food stands along the 3-mile boardwalk, and you have to try some of the famous saltwater taffy and Thrasher's french fries with vinegar.

The Ocean City restaurant that has to be a first on anyone's list is **Phillips Crab House.** The restaurant, which was started by Shirley and Brice Phillips from Hooper's Island on the Chesapeake Bay, has been an Ocean City ritual since 1956. The two of them have become such an institution and such an integral part of their community that they were honored in 1989 by the Ocean City Good Will Ambassadors Grand Ball. The restaurant has branched out to seven locations, a hotel, and eateries in Baltimore's Harborplace, Washington, D.C., and Norfolk.

But the Ocean City location is the one to visit. It was a shingle-covered shack in the boonies when it opened. Now it is in the middle of everything that is happening and can seat 1,400 diners at one time. Despite its size, you will have to arrive early or plan to wait awhile, because there is always a line for dinner. This is where you come to eat crabs, piled in mounds on broad sheets of paper that cover tables that once held sewing machines. And if steamed crabs, spiced shrimp, and crab cakes don't appeal to you, there is always fried chicken, Virginia baked ham served with corn on the cob, watermelon, and coleslaw. A children's menu is available.

Phillips Crab House is at 21st Street and Philadelphia Avenue, Ocean City 21842. For information call (301) 289-6821.

Those of you who served aboard the USS *324*, a World War II submarine that was built in 1944 and saw battle in the Java and South China seas, will find her serving a new function as a reef off Ocean City. The *Blenny* was scuttled in 1989 about 15 miles offshore. It will act as a base for algae and soft coral growth, which will attract small fish, and then larger fish, fishermen, and divers.

141

Southern Eastern Shore

Ocean City is not just for summer fun. It is a year-round community that sponsors a great number of activities during the winter season, including workshops, entertainments, an annual Christmas parade, a traditional lighting and trimming of a 30-foot tree on the beach, a 3-mile Boardwalk Parade of Trees with special evening tours on the boardwalk train (call 301–289–8559 for details), and numerous other events. A brochure about Christmas in Ocean City (as well as Berlin, Snow Hill, and Pocomoke) is available from the Ocean City Public Relations Office, P.O. Box 158, Ocean City 21842. You can call the office at (301) 289–2800.

For additional information, write or call the Maryland Lower Shore Tourist Information Center (Route 2, Box 361A, Pocomoke City 21851, 301–957–2484) or Worcester County Tourism (P.O. Box 208, Snow Hill 21863, 301–632–3617).

About the Authors

Judy and Ed Colbert are longtime residents of Maryland and have spent years traveling the state, looking for the unusual and unique. Ed is a television production manager with the U.S. government, and Judy conducts a prolific writing and photography career.

An award-winning free-lance writer and photographer, Judy covers travel primarily. Her more than 500 articles and photographs have appeared in such publications as *Washingtonian*, *Maryland*, *AAA World*, *Women's Sports & Fitness*, *Destinations*, *American Health*, *Home & Away*, *Recreation News*, *Photo District News*, *Self*, and *Frequent Flyer*. She is also considered a specialist in travel information and has appeared on "Good Morning America," Arthur Frommer's "Almanac of Travel," and numerous other radio and television programs. She is heard regularly on WMAL AM radio in Washington, D.C.

Other titles that Judy and Ed have coauthored include *The Spa Guide*, and *Virginia: Off the Beaten Path*, both published by The Globe Pequot Press.

Index

145

149

Other Books of Interest
from the Globe Pequot Press

Off the Beaten Path series

Colorado	Minnesota	Pennsylvania
Florida	North Carolina	Southern California
Georgia	Northern California	Tennessee
Illinois	New Jersey	Virginia
Indiana	New York	Wisconsin
Michigan	Ohio	

Recommended Country Inns series

Mid-Atlantic and Chesapeake Region

•

Bed & Breakfast in the Mid-Atlantic
•
*Daytrips, Getaway Weekends, and Vacations
in the Mid-Atlantic States*
•
Factory Outlet Guide to the Mid-Atlantic States
•
Hiking Virginia's National Forests
•
Walks in the Great Smokies

These and other travel and regional books are available at your bookstore or direct from the publisher. For a free catalogue, write: The Globe Pequot Press, Box Q, Chester, CT 06412, or call 1–800–243–0495. In Connecticut, call 1–800–962–0973.